PENGUIN BOOKS

CW01652750

The CSIRO and Baker IDI Diabetes Recipe Book

Baker IDI Heart and Diabetes Institute is an independent, internationally renowned medical research facility working on the diagnosis, prevention and treatment of diabetes and cardiovascular disease. The main laboratory facilities in Melbourne are complemented by a national network that includes a research facility in Alice Springs dedicated to Indigenous health and a research node in South Australia focused on community interventions and nutrition. The main areas of research are: population studies and profiling; human physiology and behavioural science; metabolism; diabetic complications; vascular biology and hypertension; and cardiology and therapeutics. The Institute also runs a multidisciplinary, evidence-based diabetes clinic, diabetes education services, and a world-class Healthy Hearts Clinic that provides cardiovascular disease risk assessments. In addition, Baker IDI trains health professionals and collaborates on international research projects into heart disease and diabetes. In line with Baker IDI's commitment to translating its research findings into better health, the Institute has established a Healthy Lifestyle Research Centre, which examines the role of nutrition, physical exercise, genetic and environmental factors in disease. For more information, visit bakeridi.edu.au or follow the Institute on Facebook or Twitter.

The CSIRO Preventative Health National Research Flagship aims to improve the health and wellbeing of Australians through the prevention and early detection of chronic disease. As populations age, preventing or delaying chronic disease is the key to improving health and wellbeing. The Flagship's research focuses on: colorectal cancer and diseases of the gut; brain health, including neurodegenerative diseases such as Alzheimer's disease; and excess weight and obesity and its associated complications, including diabetes and cardiovascular disease. The main thrust of the research is to develop better screening for and early detection of disease, better understanding of how diet and environment contribute to disease, new protective foods and personalised nutritional and lifestyle approaches to disease prevention, and better ways to monitor and measure health, incorporating improved use of health data. CSIRO is working in partnership with a range of prominent clinical, research, government and industry organisations to ensure these research findings have a positive impact on the health of all Australians. For more, visit csiro.au/org/PreventativeHealthFlagship.html

The CSIRO and BAKER IDI Diabetes Recipe Book

Photography by Cath Muscat

CSIRO
Baker IDI
HEART & DIABETES INSTITUTE

Contents

Introduction

If you have type 2 diabetes, you are not alone. More than 1.5 million Australians have diabetes, and more than twice that number are likely to develop diabetes in the next five to ten years.

The good news is that type 2 diabetes can be controlled so you can lead a normal life. The right eating plan, regular exercise and, where necessary, diabetes medication, can make all the difference.

In our first book, *The CSIRO and Baker IDI Diabetes Diet and Lifestyle Plan*, we provided a comprehensive approach to managing type 2 diabetes – from both a medical and a lifestyle perspective. That book is an essential companion to this publication – it is a 'must have' as an important information resource. This book focuses on the eating plan and provides many new and delicious recipes. We have particularly focused on higher protein recipes, as the research shows this approach may achieve better blood sugar control.

Although it is commonly believed that the diet for managing diabetes requires you to give up all the foods that you enjoy, these recipes will show that is not necessary. In fact, if you look at the daily core food allowance (see pages 12–13), you will notice that these foods are what everyone around you will be enjoying – it is the portion size that counts!

To keep your approach to a healthier lifestyle with diabetes simple, aim to:

1. Improve the quality of your diet, by including the suggested portions of fruit and vegetables, fibre-rich wholegrain cereals, low-fat dairy and by replacing animal fat with monounsaturated and polyunsaturated oils, nuts and spreads.
2. Stop weight gain, and, if you are overweight, you can use these recipes in conjunction with *The CSIRO and Baker IDI Diabetes Diet and Lifestyle Plan* to help you lose weight.
3. Be as active as possible at work and at home. Go for a walk of at least 30 minutes every day, lift some weights or stretch some bands. Don't sit down in front of the computer or TV for hours without having frequent breaks.
4. Don't smoke.
5. Follow the instructions of your doctors and healthcare team. Take all prescribed tablets and injections, and see your doctor at least twice a year for blood tests and blood pressure checks.
6. See your eye doctor, see a dietitian, have someone look at your feet regularly and have a urine test every year. Good control of your sugar levels should prevent complications in these areas from arising. Check your sugar levels regularly if your doctor has asked you to do this.

Although both type 1 and type 2 diabetes have strong genetic links, paying attention to your diet, weight and exercise patterns can make an enormous difference to your blood sugar, blood cholesterol and blood pressure levels, and keep you well and active.

The CSIRO and Baker IDI Diabetes Recipe Book works in conjunction with *The CSIRO and Baker IDI Diabetes Diet and Lifestyle Plan* to provide you with over 115 healthy, incredibly satisfying and tasty recipes using everyday foods that even those without diabetes will enjoy.

The diabetes healthy eating plan

What you choose to eat can be vitally important to your health and wellbeing. Your diet can make a tremendous difference to your blood glucose levels, your blood pressure and your cholesterol levels.

It used to be thought that a diet for controlling diabetes was all about cutting out sugar. These days, the nutritional recommendations focus more on weight control and a healthy eating pattern low in saturated fat and high in fibre, with a moderate intake of less refined wholegrain carbohydrate foods, and of healthy fats such as those in oils and nuts. A small amount of added sugar is not a problem, since we now know that starchy carbohydrate foods cause a greater increase in blood glucose levels than sugar does. The quality of the carbohydrate foods you choose and the type of fats you eat are important.

After we eat carbohydrate-rich foods such as sugar, bread, pasta, rice, fruits and cereal-based foods, the carbohydrate they contain is converted into glucose and absorbed into the bloodstream, causing blood glucose levels to rise, reaching a peak 30–60 minutes later. Eating fewer carbohydrate foods can help prevent this rise in blood glucose levels after meals without affecting your insulin resistance – but cutting out carbohydrate foods altogether is not the solution.

Different types of carbohydrate cause different responses in our blood glucose levels. The glycaemic index (GI) is a measure of that response and we recommend eating moderate amounts of lower-GI carbohydrate foods.

The eating plan in this book (see page 7) is designed for anyone who wants to improve their lifestyle, but particularly people with a family history of diabetes, high cholesterol or high blood pressure. The eating plan is adaptable for weight loss or long-term weight maintenance, and will allow you to enjoy good food while keeping your diabetes under control.

Determining your daily energy needs

You may or may not need to lose weight, so there are versions of the eating plan to suit everyone. To work out which level of the eating plan you should follow, first calculate the kilojoules (energy)

Activity factors

ACTIVITY LEVEL	DESCRIPTION	ACTIVITY FACTOR
inactive	little or no exercise each day, probably have a desk job	1.2
lightly active	light exercise or sport on 1–3 days a week	1.375
moderately active	moderate exercise or sport on 3–5 days a week	1.55
very active	hard exercise or sport on 6–7 days a week	1.725
extremely active	hard daily exercise or sport or a physical job or hard training (marathon, triathlon, etc.)	1.9

you need to maintain your current weight, or Basal Metabolic Rate (BMR). You will need to know your height in centimetres and your weight in kilograms. You will also need to select an appropriate activity factor from the table on page 4.

Women should use this equation:

[655.1 + (9.56 x weight in kg) + (1.85 x height in cm) – (4.68 x age in years)] x 4.2 x activity factor

Men should use this equation:

[66.47 + (13.75 x weight in kg) + (5 x height in cm) – (6.76 x age in years)] x 4.2 x activity factor

Example

Donna is 50 years old, 170 cm tall and weighs 78 kg. She walks her dog 2–3 times a week, giving her an activity factor of 1.375. Donna's daily energy requirements to maintain her current weight, or BMR, will be:

[655.1 + (9.56 x 78) + (1.85 x 170) – (4.68 x 50)] x 4.2 x 1.375)
= [655.1 + 745.68 + 314.5 – 234] x 5.775
= 1481.28 x 5.775
= 8554 kJ (rounded down)

Many people will find it hard to calculate their daily energy requirements (BMR) and their body mass index (BMI), so there are websites with calculators to do it for you. The Baker IDI website (bakeridi.edu.au) has calculators, or type 'BMR' or 'BMI' into your search engine.

BODY MASS INDEX (BMI)

BMI is used to measure whether you are under- or overweight or fall within the healthy range. You can calculate yours by dividing your weight in kilograms by the square of your height in metres. It is easy to calculate, but it can be misleading (see note below), so if you are worried you can always discuss your BMI with your diabetes care team.

$$\text{BMI} = \frac{\text{weight in kilograms}}{(\text{height in metres})^2}$$

Example

Donna's height in metres is 1.7 and she weighs 78 kg. Her BMI is therefore:

78 divided by 1.7 squared
$= 78/(1.7)^2 = 27$ (rounding up)

Please note: BMI measures can be misleading for children and elite athletes.

What your BMI tells you

BODY CONDITION	NON-ASIAN BMI	ASIAN* BMI
underweight	18.5 or less	18.5 or less
healthy	18.6–24.9	18.6–22.9
overweight	25–29.9	23–27.4
obese	30 or more	27.5 or more

* The term 'Asian' here covers people from the Indian subcontinent, Middle East, North Africa and Southern Europe.

YOUR DAILY KILOJOULE REQUIREMENTS FOR WEIGHT LOSS

If your BMI indicates that you need to lose weight, subtract 2000–4000 kJ from the current daily kilojoule intake you calculated above. To reduce your weight by 0.5 kg (500 g) each week, subtract 2000 kJ; to reduce your weight by 1 kg each week, subtract 4000 kJ.

Example

Donna now knows that her energy requirement (BMR) is 8554 kJ/day and that her BMI is 27, which places her in the overweight category. Donna is aiming for a small weight loss, so she reduces her kilojoule intake by 2000 kJ per day. Her daily kilojoule requirement for weight loss is:

8554 - 2000

= 6554 kJ

HOW MUCH WEIGHT SHOULD YOU LOSE?

Aiming to reach a target weight that brings you into the healthy BMI category is a guide, but this may not be easily achievable. Even a 5 per cent weight loss can improve diabetes control and may prevent diabetes in some people.

The eating plan

Opposite is a sample day for Level 2 on the eating plan. The recipes referred to are all from this book and all suit the diabetes eating plan.

CARBOHYDRATE EXCHANGES

You will notice that the sample meal plan opposite includes a column for 'carbohydrate exchanges'. This term, which we use throughout this section, means the same as carbohydrate serves, which is part of a system for counting carbohydrates.

Carbohydrates are starches and sugars found in food. They are broken down into glucose during digestion and absorbed into the bloodstream. Carbohydrates are found in a wide range of food groups such as fruits, dairy, breads and cereals (including potato, rice, pasta, noodles and

The diabetes healthy eating plan, Levels 1–4

EATING PLAN LEVEL	1	2	3	4
Total daily energy intake (kilojoules)	5500	6500	7500	8500
Protein foods (units*/day)	2	2½	3	3½
Low-GI wholegrain bread and cereals (units/day)	4	5	5	6
Reduced-fat dairy (units/day)	3	3	4	4
Fruit (units/day)	2	2	2	3
Free List vegetables and salad (minimum units/day)	5	5	5	5
Fats (nuts, seeds and oils) (units/day)	4	6	6	7
Daily carbohydrate exchanges**	8	9	10	12
Indulgence foods (units/week)	2	4	4	4

* What constitutes a unit for each food type is explained on pages 12–13

** Carbohydrate exchanges are based on 15 g of carbohydrate per unit of bread, dairy and fruit (excluding cheese), so that 1 unit of bread provides 1 carbohydrate exchange

A sample day for Level 2 (6500 kJ)

	MEAL OPTIONS	CARBOHYDRATE EXCHANGES	UNITS PROVIDED
Breakfast	40 g low-GI, high-fibre cereal (2 carbohydrate exchanges [30 g carbohydrate]) with 250 ml low-fat/skim milk (1 carbohydrate exchange)	3 exchanges	2 units bread, 1 unit dairy
Lunch	**Warm spicy chicken tortillas (see page 47)** (1 carbohydrate exchange) served with 1 cup of mixed green salad with oil-free dressing and 35 g croutons (1 carbohydrate exchange)	2 exchanges	½ unit protein, 2 units bread, 1 unit dairy, 3 units vegetables
	<u>Afternoon tea option</u> 150 g fresh fruit salad (1 carbohydrate exchange) plus 100 g reduced-fat vanilla yoghurt (½ carbohydrate exchange) and 20 g mixed seeds (e.g. chia seeds)	1½ exchanges	½ unit dairy, 1 unit fruit, 2 units fats
Dinner	**Chicken stir-fry with vegetables and rice noodles (see page 103)** (1 carbohydrate exchange)	1 exchange	2 units protein, 1 unit bread, 2 units vegetables, 2 units fats
	<u>Dessert/supper option</u> **Pineapple and mint crush with lime 'ice-cream' (see page 205)** (1½ carbohydrate exchanges)	1½ exchanges	½ unit dairy, 1 unit fruit
Total daily intake		**9 exchanges**	**2½ units protein** **5 units bread** **3 units dairy** **2 units fruit** **5 units vegetables** **4 units fats**

legumes). They are also found in many indulgence foods, including ice-cream, sweet biscuits, sugar, honey, regular soft drinks and cordials.

Healthcare professionals use carbohydrate exchanges to estimate carbohydrate intake so that people with diabetes can plan how carbohydrate-based foods are placed within their diet. Using carbohydrate exchanges and identifying which foods provide the standard carbohydrate amount (i.e. the 15 g per exchange – see box below) will give you increased flexibility when making suitable food choices.

1 carbohydrate exchange = 15 g of carbohydrate which is provided by:

- 1 unit of bread/cereal (including starchy vegetables)
- 1 unit of fruit; or
- 1 unit of dairy (excluding cheese).

It is important to understand how the carbohydrates in foods are spread across your day, as carbohydrates are the primary nutrient that affect your post-meal blood glucose levels. Having too much carbohydrate at one meal or snack can result in high blood glucose levels.

Other reasons why it is helpful to count carbohydrate exchanges are:

- for those using oral hypoglycaemic agents or insulin doses, it is important to count the carbohydrate exchanges to promote a consistent carbohydrate intake across the day and to help match the pre-meal insulin dose to the amount of carbohydrate you will be eating.
- counting carbohydrate exchanges helps you to control your overall kilojoule intake and reduce portion serves for weight loss and improved glycaemic control.

It is a good idea to speak with your dietitian or diabetes educator to help you understand the concept of carbohydrate exchanges and counting.

YOUR DAILY CORE FOOD ALLOWANCE

The following information provides you with an overview of the daily core food allowance recommended for the Diabetes Diet and Lifestyle Plan. By using the sample meal plan (see page 7) as a guide, you will become familiar with the core features of this eating plan and can work towards establishing a good routine. Recipes in this book use the portions from the core food allowances listed here, and as you become more confident with the mix of foods, you can start to be creative with your meals. It is important to include each of the required units each day, as each food group provides key nutrients and benefits.

Please see pages 12–13 for the table showing your daily core food allowance on Level 2.

THE FREE LIST:

Free List foods contain minimal carbohydrates and kilojoules, so eat them freely to spice up your meals and help control hunger.

Vegetables – all vegetables *except* potato, pumpkin, sweet corn and sweet potato.

Drinks – water, cocoa (not drinking chocolate), coffee, diet cordial, diet soft drinks, herbal tea, unflavoured mineral water and tea.

Condiments – barbecue sauce, chilli sauce, clear soup, curry powder or paste, diet jelly, diet topping, garlic, ginger, herbs, hoisin sauce, horseradish, lemon juice, low-kilojoule sweeteners, mint sauce, mustard, oil-free dressings, parsley, pickles, salt-reduced soy sauce, salt-reduced stock, spices, tomato paste, tomato salsa, tomato sauce, Vegemite, verjuice, vinegar and wasabi.

Please note: Many condiments and sauces are high in salt, so avoid these. A small amount of cornflour, custard powder or sugar is fine to thicken or sweeten dishes: 1 level teaspoon of cornflour, custard or sugar contains 40–60 kilojoules. This is low enough not to worry about if you use them only occasionally.

If nuts are used in a recipe in small amounts it is okay to consider their kilojoule contribution as negligible. Alternatively, you could treat them as part of your fat allowance.

The weight maintenance plan

Weight maintenance after weight loss can be challenging, mainly because in the relief of reaching our target weight, we often forget the healthy habits that helped us get there. Make your new eating and exercise habits a way of life from the beginning, to ensure you can maintain your healthy weight in the long term.

The people who are most successful at maintaining their weight loss are more likely to:

1. monitor their weight and food intake by using a food diary
2. maintain or seek additional support, including fitness or weight-loss groups
3. exercise regularly – at least 30 minutes, four days a week
4. accept that they are responsible for their own health
5. monitor their hunger and be aware of appropriate portion sizes
6. have three meals a day and snack on healthy foods between meals if needed
7. set small and realistic goals and review these at suitable times
8. maintain a positive attitude and get back on track after dietary lapses
9. develop interests and hobbies to help them focus on things other than food
10. develop creative ways to manage stress effectively, including seeking help.

We all have different energy needs, so there will be a period of trial and error as you work out how much you should eat to maintain your new weight. We suggest keeping to the basic structure of the eating plan and slowly adding new foods to your daily allowance in 500-kJ 'blocks', relying more frequently on the core foods – see the table on page 10 for suggestions and check food labels for kilojoule information if you want to try a food that is not listed in the table.

It's best to weigh your portions – it is easy to become complacent and underestimate the amounts we are eating.

ADDING 500-KJ BLOCKS ON THE MAINTENANCE PLAN

The idea is to add one 500-kJ block to your daily allowance each week until you are maintaining your weight. You can vary the 500-kJ blocks within the week or, if you are planning to eat out, you can save them up. Here's how to add the blocks to your daily allowance over a three-week period and beyond.

week 1	Add 1 x 500-kJ block to your basic eating plan each day.
week 2	If you're still losing weight, add another 500-kJ block to your basic eating plan each day.
week 3	If you're still losing weight, add another 500-kJ food block to your basic eating plan each day and continue doing this each week until you maintain your weight.

Sample 500-kJ blocks*

CORE FOOD GROUP	FOOD	500-KJ BLOCK	UNITS
bread	pasta	⅓ cup cooked	1 unit bread
	sweet potato	150 g	1 unit bread
	bread – wholegrain, wholemeal, fruit	1 x 35 g slice	1 unit bread
protein	tofu or TVP (textured vegetable protein)	100 g	1 unit protein
	tinned beans	150 g cooked	1 unit bread *or* 1 unit protein
	dried chickpeas or legumes	40 g	1 unit bread *or* 1 unit protein
	cooked fish, chicken, beef, lamb or turkey	100 g	1 unit protein
	boiled egg	1	½ unit protein
dairy	low-fat milk or flavoured milk	250 ml	1 unit dairy
	low-fat ice-cream	70 g	1 unit dairy
	low-fat yoghurt or custard	200 g	1 unit dairy
	Frûche or fromage frais	150 g	1 unit dairy
	full-fat cheese	10 g	1 unit dairy
	reduced-fat cheese	20 g	1 unit dairy
fruit	fresh fruit salad	300 g	2 units fruit
	unsweetened fruit juice	250 ml	2 units fruit
	dried fruit – apricot, mango	60 g	2 units fruit
fats	sunflower, pumpkin or sesame seeds	20 g	2 units fat
	tahini paste	3½ teaspoons (20 g)	1 unit fat
	light peanut butter	3½ teaspoons (20 g)	1 unit fat
	unsaturated oil	3 teaspoons	3 units fat
	dry-roasted, unsalted nuts	20 g	1 unit fat
	avocado	¼ (40 g)	2 units fat
indulgence	wine	150 ml	1 unit indulgence
	beer	375 ml	1 unit indulgence
	spirits	60 ml	2 units indulgence
	chocolate	20 g	1 unit indulgence
	crisps – potato, chickpea, pita, soya or Peaz (cooked in canola or sunola oil with no added salt)	1 x 21 g packet	1 unit indulgence
	air-popped popcorn, no added salt	4 cups	1 unit indulgence
	honey	30 ml	1 unit indulgence
	sugar	6 teaspoons (30 g)	1 unit indulgence

* Choose low- or reduced-salt options whenever possible

If you start to gain weight again, do not add any foods the following week. If your weight gain is more than 1 kg, drop back to the previous week's plan. Once you reach a stage where your weight becomes stable, that should remain your eating plan for long-term weight maintenance. You will need to weigh yourself weekly during this transition phase to judge the effect of adding extra foods to your diet. Once you have achieved a stable weight, however, weighing yourself once a fortnight at the same time and in the same state of dress or undress is more than enough.

Five weeks on the maintenance plan

week 1 maintenance	choose any 1 block, e.g. 1 x 35 g slice toast at breakfast
week 2 maintenance	choose any 2 blocks, e.g. 1 x 35 g slice toast + 20 g nuts as a snack
week 3 maintenance	choose any 3 blocks, e.g. 1 x 35 g slice toast + 20 g nuts + 20 g dark chocolate
week 4 maintenance	choose any 4 blocks, e.g. 1 x 35 g slice toast + 20 g nuts + 20 g dark chocolate + 150 ml wine
week 5 maintenance	choose any 5 blocks, e.g. 1 x 35 g slice toast + 20 g nuts + 20 g dark chocolate + 150 ml wine + 1 piece fruit

Don't forget to stay active. If you change how much you exercise, you may also need to alter your food intake. This will be the key to maintaining your healthy weight and staying in control of your diabetes forever.

Please note: Only continue to add blocks if you are still losing weight. As soon as your weight stabilises, stop adding blocks.

KEEPING A FOOD DIARY

One of the most important tools for losing weight successfully *and* maintaining weight loss in the longer term is to keep a food diary. Recording your daily food intake not only makes you more accountable and aware of what you're eating, it also helps you monitor your eating patterns and identify any problem areas that may lead to weight regain or that cause problems with your blood sugar levels.

Once you have achieved your target weight and feel in control of your eating, you will find that you don't have to monitor your intake as much. A weekly or even monthly food diary may then be enough to help you maintain your weight. If you find you are slowly regaining weight or feeling out of control with your eating, you may need to go back to recording your intake on a daily basis to get yourself back on track.

Your daily core food allowance

(Level 2 – 6500 kJ)

1 LOW-GI HIGH-FIBRE BREAD OR CEREAL FOODS

5 units a day

Note: 1 unit of the foods listed below
= 15 g carbohydrates or 1 exchange

1 unit bread provides 300–400 kJ and is equal to:

- 20 g low-GI, high-fibre breakfast cereal, e.g. Kellogg's Guardian, Komplete or Sustain; Uncle Toby's Oatbrits; untoasted natural muesli (including gluten-free); rolled oats; Freedom Quick Oats Porridge
- 1 x 35 g slice low-GI wholegrain bread
- 1 large slice fruit loaf
- 1 x 40 g slice wholewheat Mountain Bread
- ¼ cup cooked basmati rice
- ½ cup wholemeal pasta, noodles or couscous
- 100 g cooked legumes*, e.g. lentils, baked beans or any cooked bean mix
- 100 g sweet potato
- 200 g pumpkin
- 70 g sweet corn
- crispbread – 3 x Ryvita or 4 x Vita-Weat

* We recommend cooked legumes for lunch or dinner at least twice a week (counted either as a protein or carbohydrate unit)

2 LEAN PROTEIN FOODS

2½ units a day*

1 unit protein provides 500–600 kJ and is equal to:

- 100 g any raw lean meat, including fish** and chicken
- 100 g tofu
- 100 g TVP (textured vegetable protein)
- 150 g cooked legumes, e.g. lentils, baked beans or any cooked bean mix
- 2 eggs (up to 6 eggs a week)

* We suggest ½ unit at lunch and 2 units at dinner
** We recommend fish for lunch or dinner at least twice a week

3 LOW-FAT DAIRY

3 units a day

Note: 1 unit of the foods listed below (excluding cheese) = 15 g carbohydrates or 1 exchange

1 unit dairy provides 350–450 kJ and is equal to:

- 250 ml skim, low-fat or soy milk
- 200 g low-fat, diet or soy yoghurt, e.g. Nestlé diet or Yoplait formé
- 200 g low-fat custard or dairy dessert
- 20 g reduced-fat (less than 10 per cent) cheese
- 10 g full-fat cheese

4 FRUIT

2 units a day

Note: 1 unit of the foods listed below = 15 g carbohydrates or 1 exchange

1 unit fruit provides 250–350 kJ and is equal to:

- 150 g fresh or tinned, unsweetened fruit
- 150 ml unsweetened fruit juice
- 30 g dried fruit

5 VEGETABLES

At least 5 units a day from the Free List (see page 8)

1 unit vegetables provides 80–100 kJ and is equal to 1 cup cooked vegetables

We recommend ½ unit salad and 2 units cooked vegetables each day. Aim to include orange and green vegetables, such as carrots, spinach and broccoli, to boost your intake of a range of nutrients.

6 FATS (NUTS, SEEDS AND OILS)

Up to 6 units a day

1 unit fats provides 200–250 kJ and is equal to:

- 1 teaspoon any liquid oil, such as canola, olive, grapeseed or sunflower oil
- 1 teaspoon polyunsaturated or monounsaturated margarine
- 2 teaspoons fat-reduced polyunsaturated or monounsaturated (light) margarine
- 10 g nuts or seeds
- 20 g avocado

7 INDULGENCE FOODS

4 units a week*

1 unit indulgence is equal to any food or drink providing approximately 450 kJ, such as 150 ml wine or 20 g chocolate.

*If you are aiming to lose weight, you may wish to make this 2 units a week

If you don't need to lose weight, you can be more liberal with your core foods, including nuts, seeds, fruit, cereals and low-fat dairy foods.

Breakfasts and snacks

1 SERVE =
¾ UNIT DAIRY
1 UNIT FRUIT

Peach and pineapple lassi

SERVES 4 PREP TIME **5 minutes**

A lassi is a traditional Indian yoghurt drink that can be served plain, sweet or salty. It's ideal for breakfast, but also the perfect drink to cool you down on a hot day.

2 peaches, roughly chopped
300 g pineapple flesh (or 2 × 225 g tins pineapple chunks or rings in juice, drained, juice discarded), roughly chopped
600 g reduced-fat Greek-style yoghurt
finely grated zest of 1 lime
2 tablespoons lime juice
8 ice cubes, crushed

1 Place all the ingredients (except the ice) in a blender and process until smooth.

2 Divide the crushed ice among four glasses, pour over the lassi and serve immediately or allow to chill over the ice for 5 minutes.

TIP If you prefer the peaches peeled, score a cross in the base of each peach, then place in a bowl of boiling water for 30 seconds. Immediately plunge into cold water, then remove and peel off the skin. Note that some peach varieties are difficult to peel.

1 SERVE =
¾ UNIT DAIRY
1 UNIT FRUIT

Mango and strawberry smoothie

SERVES 4 PREP TIME **10 minutes**

A quick and easy breakfast for when you're in a hurry. This smoothie is rich and thick, so if you prefer, add a little extra reduced-fat milk to thin it down.

1 large ripe mango, flesh roughly chopped
6 strawberries, hulled and halved
1½ cups (375 ml) reduced-fat milk
300 g reduced-fat natural yoghurt
2 teaspoons honey or Splenda
2 tablespoons wheat germ

1 Place all the ingredients in a blender and process until smooth.

2 Divide among four glasses and serve immediately.

L: Peach and Pineapple Lassi; R: Mango and Strawberry Smoothie

1 SERVE =
1 UNIT BREAD
½ UNIT DAIRY
1 UNIT FRUIT
1 UNIT FATS

Overnight muesli with apple, pear and nuts

SERVES 4 PREP TIME **10 minutes**

Now there's no excuse for missing out on a healthy breakfast – spend 10 minutes the night before preparing this muesli, then all you have to do in the morning is serve it up.

2 apples, grated, including skin
2 pears, grated, including skin
250 g reduced-fat thick natural yoghurt
¾ cup (65 g) wholegrain rolled oats
2 tablespoons chopped raw hazelnuts
2 tablespoons chopped raw almonds
½ cup (125 ml) reduced-fat milk (optional)

1 Combine all the ingredients (except the milk) in a bowl, then cover and refrigerate overnight.

2 In the morning, give the muesli a quick stir, then serve, with a little reduced-fat milk stirred in if the muesli is too thick.

1 SERVE (1 SLICE) =
1 UNIT BREAD
1 UNIT FATS
¼ UNIT FRUIT

Pear and raspberry loaf

MAKES 1 × 800 G LOAF (12 SLICES)
PREP TIME **15 minutes** COOKING TIME **50 minutes**

This is delicious for morning tea. You could also wrap a slice in baking paper and take it to work as a lunchtime treat, or enjoy it as the perfect afternoon pick-me-up.

200 g (1⅓ cups) wholemeal stoneground self-raising flour
pinch salt
½ teaspoon bicarbonate of soda
4 tablespoons Splenda
2 eggs, lightly beaten
3 tablespoons vegetable oil
220 ml reduced-fat milk
2 ripe pears, peeled, cored and finely diced
½ cup (60 g) frozen raspberries

1 Preheat the oven to 180°C. Grease and line a 22 cm × 8 cm loaf tin.

2 Sift the flour into a bowl (returning any husks to the bowl) and add the salt, bicarbonate of soda and Splenda.

3 In a separate bowl, whisk together the egg, oil and milk. Add to the dry ingredients and mix to combine. Gently fold in the pear and raspberries until just mixed through – do not over-mix.

4 Spoon the batter into the prepared tin and bake for 50 minutes or until risen and golden brown. Leave to cool in the tin for 10 minutes, then carefully transfer to a wire rack and cool completely. Slice to serve.

1 SERVE =
1 UNIT PROTEIN
1 UNIT BREAD
1 UNIT DAIRY
1 UNIT VEGETABLES
1 UNIT FATS

Mushroom, ricotta and herb omelette

SERVES 4 PREP TIME **15 minutes** COOKING TIME **15 minutes**

1 tablespoon olive oil
250 g mushrooms, wiped and roughly chopped
1 clove garlic, crushed
⅓ cup (80 g) reduced-fat ricotta
2 tablespoons finely chopped flat-leaf parsley
1 tablespoon snipped chives, plus extra to garnish
8 eggs
chopped red chilli, to garnish (optional)
4 thick slices wholegrain low-GI bread, toasted

Elevate the humble mushroom with the addition of chilli and garlic. Served inside a fluffy omelette with some creamy, reduced-fat ricotta, this is a great way to start your day.

1 Heat 2 teaspoons of the oil in a medium-sized non-stick frying pan (or omelette pan). Add the mushroom and garlic and fry for 4–5 minutes or until the mushroom is cooked. Transfer to a bowl. Wipe out the pan.

2 Combine the ricotta with the parsley and chives and season with freshly ground black pepper. Set aside.

3 Beat two eggs together. Heat ½ teaspoon oil in the frying pan, add the beaten egg and cook, stirring, for 1 minute until just starting to set. Continue to cook, gently pulling the egg away from the sides and tilting the pan so the uncooked egg runs to the base and sides, until the egg is just set. Carefully spread a quarter of the ricotta mixture over one side of the omelette, then scatter a quarter of the mushroom mixture on top.

4 To serve, slide the omelette onto a plate and fold the other side over. Keep warm, and repeat with the remaining ingredients to make four omelettes. Garnish with chilli and extra chives, if liked, and serve with toast on the side.

TIPS

These mushrooms are a great addition to poached eggs, or simply piled on top of a piece of low-GI toast.

This omelette is also delicious for dinner served with steamed zucchini (courgette), asparagus and snowpeas (mange-tout).

1 SERVE =
½ UNIT PROTEIN
1 UNIT BREAD
½ UNIT DAIRY
¾ UNIT FRUIT
½ UNIT FATS

French toast with grilled stone fruit

SERVES 4 PREP TIME **20 minutes** COOKING TIME **10 minutes**

2 peaches or nectarines, halved and stones removed
4 eggs, lightly beaten
2 tablespoons reduced-fat milk
¼ cup (70 g) reduced-fat Greek-style yoghurt, plus 300 g extra to serve
large pinch ground cinnamon
4 thick slices wholegrain low-GI bread
2 teaspoons olive oil spread or other reduced-fat spread
150 g strawberries, hulled and halved

A favourite with kids and adults alike, French toast is a treat for breakfast. It's vital to use ripe fruit, otherwise it will be crunchy and lack flavour.

1 Preheat the oven grill to high and grill the peaches or nectarines, cut-side up, for 2–3 minutes or until starting to brown. Alternatively, preheat a chargrill pan and line with a piece of baking paper. Add the peaches or nectarines, cut-side down, and cook until grill marks appear. Set aside.

2 Meanwhile, combine the eggs, milk, yoghurt and cinnamon in a shallow dish. Dip each slice of bread into the egg mixture, allowing the liquid to soak in, then remove and gently shake to allow any excess to drip off.

3 Melt half the reduced-fat spread in a large non-stick frying pan over medium heat. Add two pieces of bread and cook for 2 minutes. Turn over and cook for a further 1–2 minutes or until golden. Transfer to a plate, then cover and keep warm while cooking the remaining bread in the remaining spread.

4 Serve the French toast immediately with the peach or nectarine halves, strawberries and a dollop of yoghurt.

TIP Instead of grilled stone fruit, try topping the French toast with a berry combination – blueberries, strawberries and raspberries are delicious. Or, for a very quick alternative, top with sliced banana.

1 SERVE =
½ UNIT PROTEIN
1 UNIT BREAD
½ UNIT VEGETABLES
1 UNIT FATS

Marinated mushrooms with poached eggs

SERVES 4 PREP TIME **10 minutes** COOKING TIME **15 minutes**

4 eggs
2 teaspoons sesame oil
2 teaspoons canola or olive oil
300 g chestnut or cap mushrooms, wiped and quartered (or chopped if large)
1 clove garlic, crushed
2 tablespoons salt-reduced soy sauce
2 tablespoons sherry or marsala
4 thick slices wholegrain low-GI bread, toasted
watercress sprigs, to serve

The addition of thick toast makes this a wonderfully substantial brunch, but by all means leave the bread out for a light but filling breakfast.

1 Use an egg poacher to poach the eggs, if you have one. Alternatively use the following method (you may find it easier to poach two eggs at a time, rather than all four at once). Fill a deep frying pan or wide saucepan with water about 7.5 cm deep and bring to the boil. Meanwhile, break each egg into a saucer or small ramekin. Once the water is boiling, use a wooden spoon to stir the water vigorously to form a vortex (this will help shape the eggs). Quickly slide the eggs into the vortex, then reduce the heat so the water is just simmering and poach for 3–4 minutes. Lift the eggs out with a slotted spoon and drain briefly on paper towel.

2 Meanwhile, heat the oils in a frying pan over medium heat. Add the mushroom and garlic and cook for 3–4 minutes. Add the soy sauce, sherry or marsala and plenty of freshly ground black pepper and simmer for a further 2 minutes.

3 Place a piece of toast on each plate and top with the mushroom mixture, followed by a few sprigs of watercress and a poached egg. If you like, finish with a grinding of freshly ground black pepper.

1 SERVE =
1 UNIT BREAD
¼ UNIT DAIRY
1 UNIT VEGETABLES
1¾ UNITS FATS

Mushroom bruschetta with gremolata and baby spinach

SERVES 4 PREP TIME **20 minutes** COOKING TIME **10 minutes**

4 thick slices wholegrain low-GI bread
2 teaspoons olive oil
1 large clove garlic, halved
400 g mixed mushrooms, thickly sliced
150 g baby spinach leaves
80 g reduced-fat cream cheese

GREMOLATA
finely grated zest of 1 lemon
1 clove garlic, crushed
2 tablespoons finely chopped flat-leaf parsley
1 teaspoon olive oil

Mushrooms contain large amounts of essential minerals, including potassium and selenium. For this dish, look out for the more flavourful types, including chestnut and the large portobello, which have a great, almost meaty texture. Serve the mushrooms as soon after cooking as possible, as they lose their heat quickly.

1 To make the gremolata, combine all the ingredients and some freshly ground black pepper in a bowl. Set aside.

2 Brush the bread slices with 1 teaspoon of the oil and rub all over with the cut side of the garlic clove. Set aside.

3 Heat the remaining oil in a large frying pan. Add the mushrooms and cook, stirring regularly, for 4–5 minutes or until softened and cooked. Add to the gremolata and toss to ensure the mushrooms are well coated. Cover to keep warm.

4 Briefly wash the baby spinach and place in the frying pan with only the water clinging to the leaves (no extra water). Stir-fry over medium–high heat for 1 minute until wilted. Add the cream cheese, season well with freshly ground black pepper and cook briefly until the cheese starts to melt.

5 Meanwhile, preheat the oven grill to high (or use a chargrill pan if you prefer). Grill the bread on both sides until lightly toasted.

6 Place a piece of bruschetta on each plate. Top with the spinach and cheese, then the mushroom and gremolata mixture, and serve immediately.

1 SERVE =
2 UNITS BREAD
¾ UNIT DAIRY
½ UNIT FRUIT
1 UNIT FATS

Cinnamon porridge with stewed pear and nuts

SERVES 4 PREP TIME **10 minutes**
COOKING TIME **10 minutes**

Porridge is the perfect way to warm your tummy on a cold winter's day. Make sure you use wholegrain rolled oats, not quick-cook or instant oats.

2 ripe pears, peeled, cored and chopped
1½ cups (135 g) wholegrain rolled oats
2 cups (500 ml) reduced-fat milk
¼ teaspoon ground cinnamon
100 g reduced-fat Greek-style yoghurt
2 tablespoons raw pistachio kernels
2 tablespoons chopped raw almonds

1. Place the pears in a small saucepan, then cover and cook over medium heat for 4–5 minutes. Stir gently to break up the fruit, then cook for a further 4–5 minutes until softened.
2. Meanwhile, put the oats into a saucepan with the milk and cinnamon and bring to a simmer over low heat. Simmer for 5 minutes, stirring occasionally. Add a little water if the porridge is too thick.
3. Spoon the porridge into four bowls. Top with the stewed pear and a dollop of yoghurt and scatter the nuts on top.

TIPS

Try replacing the stewed pear with stewed apple, adding 1 tablespoon water during cooking to help the apples soften.

It's worth making a batch of stewed fruit so you always have some on hand. Freeze in small portions, then thaw as you need it. Reheat the stewed fruit before serving it with the porridge.

1 SERVE =
½ UNIT PROTEIN
½ UNIT VEGETABLES
2 UNITS FATS

Avocado omelette wraps

SERVES 4 PREP TIME **10 minutes**
COOKING TIME **8 minutes**

These wraps are an ideal snack if you're trying to eat less bread. It's vital to use a non-stick pan as no additional fat is used to cook the omelettes. Try and keep them really thin to ensure easy rolling.

4 eggs, lightly beaten
2 spring onions, finely chopped
1 tablespoon snipped chives
80 g reduced-fat cream cheese
large handful rocket leaves
80 g avocado (about ½ an avocado), cut into 12 long slices

1. Whisk the eggs with 1½ tablespoons cold water in a jug. Add the spring onion and chives and whisk again.
2. Heat a non-stick frying pan over low–medium heat. Pour in just enough egg mixture to coat the base of the pan, swirling it around to form a thin omelette. Cook until it has just set, about 1 minute. Carefully turn the omelette over (it's probably easiest to use your fingers) and briefly cook the other side. Carefully slide onto a board, then cook the remaining wraps.
3. Spread each wrap with cream cheese and scatter over some rocket leaves. Arrange a line of avocado along the centre of each wrap, then roll up. Slice in half on the diagonal and serve.

TIPS

Get creative with your fillings. Try diced tomato mixed with chopped basil or cucumber batons with watercress.

For a more substantial breakfast, serve with a slice of wholegrain low-GI bread. For brunch, serve with a green salad or tomato salad on the side.

1 SERVE =
1 UNIT PROTEIN
1 UNIT DAIRY
1 UNIT VEGETABLES

Mini herb and zucchini frittatas

MAKES 12 PREP TIME **20 minutes**
COOKING TIME **30 minutes**

You will need a twelve-hole regular muffin tray to make these lovely little frittatas. So easy to whip up, they are the perfect savoury option for a light breakfast or brunch.

2 large zucchinis (courgettes), diced
4 spring onions, finely chopped
80 g reduced-fat feta, finely chopped
8 eggs
3 tablespoons reduced-fat milk
3 tablespoons finely chopped herbs, such as chives, flat-leaf parsley and basil
mixed salad leaves, to serve

1 Preheat the oven to 180°C. Cut small rounds of baking paper and line the base of each muffin hole.

2 Steam the zucchini for 4–5 minutes or until tender. Transfer to a bowl, add the spring onion and feta and mix gently. Spoon evenly into the muffin holes.

3 Whisk together the eggs, milk and herbs and season well with freshly ground black pepper. Pour the mixture into each hole until about three-quarters full. Press the vegetables down gently into the egg, if necessary.

4 Bake for 20–25 minutes or until golden and set. Leave in the tin for 5 minutes, then carefully slide a knife around the edge of each frittata and turn out. Serve warm with a mixed salad.

TIP Instead of zucchini, you could add diced, steamed sweet potato, or try a mixture of both.

1 SERVE =
¼ UNIT PROTEIN
2 UNITS BREAD
½ UNIT DAIRY
1 UNIT FRUIT
1 UNIT FATS

Banana buttermilk pancakes with strawberries ›

SERVES 4 PREP TIME **10 minutes**
COOKING TIME **15 minutes**

Pancakes are always a treat for breakfast, and these ones are healthy so they are guilt-free.

1½ cups (375 ml) buttermilk
2 eggs
1 cup (160 g) wholemeal stoneground self-raising flour
2 large ripe bananas, mashed
1 tablespoon canola or vegetable oil
100 g strawberries, hulled and halved
100 g reduced-fat vanilla or natural yoghurt

1 Whisk together the buttermilk and eggs in a bowl. Gradually whisk in the flour, then fold in the mashed banana.

2 Heat ½ teaspoon oil in a non-stick frying pan over medium–high heat. Working in batches, spoon 3 tablespoons batter per pancake into the pan to form a round about 10 cm in diameter. Cook for 2 minutes or until golden underneath and bubbles start to appear on the surface. Carefully turn over and cook for a further 1–2 minutes or until golden and risen. Remove and cover to keep warm while you make the remaining pancakes (you should have enough batter to make eight in all). Add additional oil only when required – it may not be necessary for every batch.

3 Serve the pancakes warm, with strawberries and a spoonful of yoghurt.

1 SERVE =
½ UNIT PROTEIN
1 UNIT BREAD
1 UNIT VEGETABLES
1 UNIT FATS

Tofu and sweet-corn cakes with roasted tomatoes

SERVES 4 PREP TIME **20 minutes** COOKING TIME **30 minutes**

- **2 corn cobs or 280 g frozen corn kernels, thawed**
- **2 eggs, lightly beaten**
- **200 g silken tofu**
- **2 tablespoons chopped coriander**
- **½ cup (80 g) wholemeal stoneground plain flour**
- **3 tablespoons reduced-fat milk**
- **2 spring onions, finely chopped**
- **2 teaspoons canola or olive oil**
- **rocket salad, to serve (optional)**

ROASTED TOMATOES

- **2 teaspoons olive oil**
- **1 tablespoon balsamic vinegar**
- **1 clove garlic, crushed**
- **4 tomatoes, halved lengthways**

Everybody loves corn cakes. Tofu is low in fat and an excellent source of protein, and makes these traditional favourites wonderfully light.

1. To make the roasted tomatoes, preheat the oven to 170°C. Combine the oil, balsamic vinegar and garlic in a small bowl and season well with freshly ground black pepper. Place the tomatoes on a baking tray and brush with the balsamic mixture. Bake for 30 minutes or until softened and starting to blacken. Remove from the oven.
2. Meanwhile, if using fresh corn cobs, carefully remove the kernels by slicing down the length of each cob with a sharp knife.
3. Whisk together the beaten egg, tofu, coriander, flour and milk in a large bowl and season well with freshly ground black pepper. Fold in the corn kernels and spring onions.
4. Heat 1 teaspoon oil in a large non-stick frying pan over medium heat. Spoon in a heaped tablespoon of batter for each cake, allowing enough space for spreading – you should fit six in the pan, but take care not to overcrowd it. Cook for 2 minutes, then carefully turn over and cook for a further 1–2 minutes or until golden. Repeat with the remaining batter and oil to make twelve corn cakes.
5. Serve three corn cakes per person with the roasted tomatoes and rocket salad, if you like.

TIP If you like a bit of heat, try adding one seeded and finely chopped chilli to the batter.

Lunches and light meals

1 SERVE =
½ UNIT PROTEIN
2 UNITS DAIRY
2 UNITS VEGETABLES
1 UNIT FATS

Baked ricotta and zucchini slice with tomato and herb salad

SERVES 4 PREP TIME **20 minutes** COOKING TIME **30 minutes**

160 g reduced-fat ricotta
4 eggs, lightly beaten
1 tablespoon lemon juice
2 tablespoons chopped flat-leaf parsley
2 zucchinis (courgettes), grated
4 tablespoons pitted black olives, finely chopped
30 g sun-dried tomatoes, drained, finely chopped

TOMATO AND HERB SALAD
4 firm, ripe tomatoes, roughly chopped
100 g mixed salad leaves
small handful mint leaves
3 teaspoons olive oil
1 tablespoon lemon juice

This slice can be made in advance, ready to share at a picnic or brunch, or you could wrap slices in baking paper and take to school or work as a packed lunch.

1. Preheat the oven to 180°C. Grease a 20 cm × 9 cm loaf tin and line the base with baking paper.
2. Combine the ricotta, eggs, lemon juice and parsley in a bowl and season with freshly ground black pepper. Add the zucchini, olives and sun-dried tomatoes and mix well. Spoon into the prepared tin and smooth the top, then bake for 30 minutes or until firm.
3. Leave to cool in the tin for 10 minutes, then carefully run a knife around the edges and turn out onto a wire rack or board.
4. Meanwhile, to make the salad, combine the tomatoes, salad leaves and mint in a bowl. Drizzle over the oil and lemon juice, season with freshly ground black pepper and mix well.
5. Cut the slice into fingers and serve warm or chilled with the salad.

1 SERVE =
½ UNIT PROTEIN
1 UNIT BREAD
2 UNITS VEGETABLES

Prawn and vegetable rice paper rolls

SERVES 4 PREP TIME **45 minutes**

60 g rice vermicelli noodles
8 × 22 cm round rice paper wrappers
8 large mint leaves
16 coriander leaves
16 (200 g) cooked and peeled king prawns, halved lengthways
1 small carrot, cut into sixteen batons
1 small red capsicum (pepper), trimmed, seeded and cut into sixteen batons
8 snowpeas (mange-tout), sliced lengthways into thirds

These can be made a few hours in advance – just keep them covered with damp paper towels and store them in the fridge until needed. Or, if you prefer, put all the ingredients out on the table and let everyone help themselves, filling and rolling their own.

1 Soak the noodles in a large bowl of boiling water for 5 minutes or until softened. Drain and rinse under cold water, then drain again and set aside.

2 Fill a large bowl with hot (not boiling) water and dip a rice paper wrapper into the water briefly, until it is pliable but not too soft. This will take between 10 and 30 seconds. Let any excess water drip off, then carefully lay on a plate. Repeat with the remaining wrappers. The wrappers are quite robust, but be careful not to tear them.

3 Place one mint leaf and two coriander leaves down the centre of the wrapper, leaving about 2 cm at each end. Place four pieces of prawn on top and then some noodles. Top with two carrot and two capsicum batons and three slices of snowpea. Fold in the ends of the wrapper then, starting from one side, roll up tightly to enclose the filling.

4 Place the rice paper roll on a plate, seam-side down, and cover with a piece of damp paper towel while you make the rest. Serve two rolls per person.

TIP You can vary the filling in these rolls to suit your taste. Swap the prawn for cooked chicken, or try adding a handful of bean sprouts, cucumber batons or some shredded lettuce.

1 SERVE =
½ UNIT PROTEIN
2 UNITS BREAD
2 UNITS VEGETABLES
2 UNITS FATS

Tabouli, hummus and crunchy vegetable pitas

SERVES 4 PREP TIME **30 minutes, plus soaking and cooling time**
COOKING TIME **1 hour**

4 low-GI wholemeal pita breads
2 Lebanese (small) cucumbers, diced
2 carrots, grated

HUMMUS

120 g dried chickpeas, washed and soaked overnight in cold water
2 teaspoons tahini
1 clove garlic, crushed
2–3 tablespoons lemon juice
1 tablespoon finely chopped flat-leaf parsley

TABOULI

½ cup (80 g) burghul (cracked wheat)
1 bunch flat-leaf parsley, finely chopped
½ bunch radishes, trimmed and finely diced
2 spring onions, finely chopped
2 tomatoes, quartered, seeded and finely diced
1½ tablespoons olive oil
2 tablespoons lemon juice

It's preferable to use dried chickpeas and soak them overnight in cold water, but if time is against you, use 200 g tinned chickpeas instead. Drain and rinse well, then proceed with step 3, adding cold water to loosen the puree as necessary.

1 To make the hummus, drain the soaked chickpeas. Place in a large saucepan and cover with about 5 cm water (do not add salt). Bring to the boil, then reduce the heat and simmer for 50–60 minutes or until very soft (this could even take a bit longer), skimming off any froth from the surface. Drain, reserving the cooking liquid, then leave to cool for 20 minutes. Remove any loose skins.

2 Meanwhile, to make the tabouli, place the burghul in a bowl and cover with water. Leave for 40 minutes or until the grains have plumped up, then drain well and transfer to a large bowl. Add the remaining ingredients, season with freshly ground black pepper and combine well. Cover and place in the fridge for at least 1 hour to allow the flavours to mingle.

3 Place the cooked chickpeas in a food processor. Add the tahini and garlic and process briefly. With the motor running, gradually add the lemon juice and enough of the reserved cooking water to form a smooth, creamy puree. (If you are using tinned chickpeas, add cold water.) Transfer to a bowl and stir in the parsley.

4 Lightly toast the pita bread, then serve with the cucumbers, carrots, hummus and tabouli.

TIP The hummus can be made in advance. It may, however, thicken on standing, so leave it in the food processor and give it a final whiz before serving, adding a bit more water if needed.

1 SERVE =
½ UNIT PROTEIN
1½ UNITS BREAD
1½ UNITS VEGETABLES
1½ UNITS FATS

Chargrilled tofu, soba noodle and pickled ginger salad

SERVES 4 PREP TIME **25 minutes, plus marinating time**
COOKING TIME **20 minutes**

120 g soba noodles
½ small red onion, thinly sliced
30 g pine nuts, toasted
3 sticks celery, thinly sliced
1 small red capsicum (pepper), trimmed, seeded and sliced
2 tablespoons pickled ginger, sliced
3 teaspoons olive oil
juice of ½ lemon

CHARGRILLED TOFU
1 tablespoon mirin
1 tablespoon salt-reduced soy sauce
1 clove garlic, crushed
250 g firm tofu

The tofu in this light, fragrant salad really benefits from being marinated, so, if you can, start this recipe a few hours ahead.

1 To prepare the tofu, combine the mirin, soy sauce and garlic and season with plenty of freshly ground black pepper. Place the tofu in a shallow bowl and pour over the marinade, turning it several times to coat. Cover and marinate in the fridge for at least 1 hour and up to 12 hours.

2 Meanwhile, cook the soba noodles in boiling water for 4 minutes or according to the packet instructions. Drain, return to the pan and pour cold water over them. Leave for 2 minutes to cool down, then drain again and place in a large bowl. Add the onion, pine nuts, celery, capsicum and ginger and toss to combine.

3 Whisk together the oil and lemon juice and season with freshly ground black pepper. Pour the dressing over the noodle salad and toss well to combine.

4 Preheat a chargrill pan over medium–high heat. Remove the tofu from the marinade and pat dry. Add to the pan and chargrill for 6–7 minutes on each side, then thinly slice.

5 Serve the noodle salad in a shallow dish with the sliced tofu arranged on top.

TIPS

The tofu can also be cooked on a hot barbecue grill plate – just make sure it is oiled or the tofu may stick.

This recipe also works beautifully with grilled chicken infused with the same marinade.

1 SERVE =
½ UNIT PROTEIN
2 UNITS VEGETABLES
½ UNIT FATS

Grilled salmon with crunchy cabbage salad

SERVES 4 PREP TIME **25 minutes** COOKING TIME **4 minutes**

olive oil, for brushing
200 g salmon fillet, skin removed and pin-boned, cut into four long thin pieces

CRUNCHY CABBAGE SALAD
½ Chinese cabbage
handful radicchio leaves, shredded
130 g snowpeas (mange-tout), sliced lengthways
30 g snowpea (mange-tout) sprouts
large handful coriander leaves, plus extra to garnish (optional)
2 teaspoons olive oil
1½ tablespoons lime juice
1 teaspoon finely grated ginger

This is a light and zesty salad, perfect for a summer lunch.

1 To make the salad, remove and discard the core from the cabbage and shred the leaves, slicing across the cabbage. Place in a large bowl with the radicchio, snowpeas, sprouts and coriander and toss to combine. Add the oil, lime juice and ginger and toss gently for 30 seconds to ensure that all the leaves are well coated. Place in the fridge while preparing the fish.

2 Preheat the oven grill to high. Line a grill tray with foil and brush lightly with oil. Cook the salmon for 2 minutes on each side or until just cooked through. Take care not to overcook or the fish will become dry.

3 Carefully slice the salmon on the diagonal and serve on a bed of crunchy cabbage salad, garnished with extra coriander leaves, if you like.

TIPS

You could use other fish fillets, such as flathead or ling, instead of salmon. Or try an oily fish such as mackerel, which is a very good source of omega-3 polyunsaturated fatty acids. If grilling whole mackerel, cook on each side for 8–10 minutes or until cooked through.

This salad is also delicious with prawns tossed through. Replace the salmon with 200 g cooked, peeled prawns.

1 SERVE =
½ UNIT PROTEIN
½ UNIT DAIRY
2 UNITS VEGETABLES
1 UNIT FATS

Indian chickpea and vegetable curry

SERVES 4 PREP TIME **20 minutes** COOKING TIME **35 minutes**

1 tablespoon vegetable oil
1 large onion, chopped
2 cloves garlic, crushed
1 green chilli, thinly sliced
1 teaspoon finely grated ginger (optional)
2 teaspoons ground cumin
2 teaspoons ground coriander
1 teaspoon ground ginger
2 zucchinis (courgettes), quartered lengthways and cut into 1 cm pieces
200 g button mushrooms, quartered
300 g tinned chickpeas, rinsed and drained
1 × 400 g tin chopped tomatoes
handful coriander leaves
400 g reduced-fat natural yoghurt

This is a delicious one-pot meal – all that's needed is a little yoghurt on the side. Although it uses a whole green chilli, it's quite a mild curry.

1. Heat the oil in a large heavy-based saucepan over medium heat. Add the onion and cook for 10 minutes, stirring regularly. Add the garlic, chilli and fresh ginger (if using) and cook for 1 minute. Add the ground spices and cook for 1 minute. Add the zucchini and mushrooms and stir to coat in the mixture, then cook for 2 minutes.
2. Add the chickpeas and tomatoes. Pour 1 cup (250 ml) water into the tomato tin and swirl it around, then add to the pan. Bring to the boil, then reduce the heat to low and simmer, covered, for 15 minutes. If the curry is too runny, take the lid off and cook for a further 5 minutes until reduced.
3. Scatter the coriander leaves over the curry and serve with a dollop of yoghurt.

1 SERVE =
½ UNIT PROTEIN
1 UNIT BREAD
1½ UNITS VEGETABLES
2 UNITS FATS

Mediterranean rice pilaf with tofu

SERVES 4 PREP TIME **15 minutes** COOKING TIME **40 minutes**

1 tablespoon finely chopped basil
1 tablespoon finely chopped oregano *or* 1 teaspoon dried oregano
2 cloves garlic, crushed
2 tablespoons olive oil
200 g firm tofu, cut into 1–2 cm cubes
1 onion, finely chopped
1 red capsicum (pepper), trimmed, seeded and diced
2 zucchinis (courgettes), diced
80 g basmati rice
1½ cups (375 ml) salt-reduced vegetable stock
lemon wedges, to serve

Use firm rather than silken tofu for this dish so it will hold its shape.

1. Combine the basil, oregano, half the garlic and 1 tablespoon of the oil in a bowl. Add the tofu and gently toss to coat. Set aside.
2. Heat the remaining oil in a large frying pan or heavy-based saucepan over medium heat and cook the onion, capsicum and remaining garlic for 5 minutes. Add the zucchini and cook for a further 5 minutes.
3. Stir in the rice and cook for 1 minute. Add the stock and season well with freshly ground black pepper. Give it another stir and bring to the boil, then reduce the heat and simmer, covered, for 25 minutes or until the rice is almost cooked. Remove the lid and gently stir in the tofu and marinade. Cook for a further 5 minutes, adjusting the heat as needed to keep the rice simmering.
4. Serve with lemon wedges for squeezing over the top.

1 SERVE =
½ UNIT PROTEIN
1 UNIT BREAD
¼ UNIT DAIRY
1½ UNITS VEGETABLES
2 UNITS FATS

Mushrooms with chicken, couscous and mint yoghurt sauce

SERVES 4 PREP TIME **30 minutes** COOKING TIME **20 minutes**

80 g couscous
2 tablespoons olive oil
1 tablespoon lemon juice
2 tablespoons finely chopped flat-leaf parsley
2 tablespoons finely chopped coriander
200 g lean minced chicken
8 large field or portobello mushrooms, wiped
2 tomatoes, each cut into four thick slices
salad leaves, to serve (optional)

MINT YOGHURT SAUCE
200 g reduced-fat Greek-style yoghurt
2 tablespoons finely shredded mint

Just the thing for days when you want something other than a sandwich for lunch, these stuffed mushrooms are filling, nutritious and taste great.

1 To make the sauce, combine the yoghurt and mint in a small bowl, and set aside to allow the flavours to develop.

2 Meanwhile, bring 100 ml water to the boil in a small saucepan. Add the couscous and fork through the grains to separate them. Remove the pan from the heat, cover and leave to stand for 2 minutes. Return the pan to a very low heat, add 2 teaspoons of the oil and cook for 3 minutes, continuing to fork through the grains. Remove from the heat and stir the grains gently. Add the lemon juice, parsley, coriander and another 2 teaspoons of oil and season well with freshly ground black pepper. Set aside for 10 minutes.

3 Heat the remaining oil in a frying pan over high heat, add the chicken mince and cook for 5 minutes or until it is cooked through, stirring regularly to break up any lumps. Add to the couscous and stir well to combine.

4 Preheat the oven grill to high. Remove and discard the mushroom stems. Grill the mushrooms, cup-side down, for 5 minutes.

5 Turn the mushrooms over and grill for 2 minutes, then top each one with a slice of tomato and grill for another 2 minutes. Pile some of the couscous onto each mushroom and serve with the mint yoghurt sauce, salad leaves (if using) and any remaining couscous.

1 SERVE =
½ UNIT PROTEIN
1 UNIT BREAD
1 UNIT VEGETABLES
1 UNIT FATS

Warm and spicy chicken tortillas

SERVES 4 PREP TIME **15 minutes** COOKING TIME **15 minutes**

⅓ cup (80 g) reduced-fat sour cream
2 tablespoons chopped coriander leaves
4 low-GI tortillas
80 g (4 slices) reduced-fat Swiss cheese, halved
200 g cooked skinless chicken breast fillet, sliced
160 g mild tomato salsa
40 g jalapeno chillies, drained and roughly chopped
rocket leaves, to serve

These are delicious served warm; they can also be prepared in advance and taken on a picnic or in a packed lunch. It's important to wrap them well before cooking, otherwise the filling may seep out. For a milder filling, reduce the amount of chilli.

1. Preheat the oven to 180°C.
2. Combine the sour cream and coriander and season well with freshly ground black pepper. Spread evenly over the tortillas, then add the cheese slices, arranging them up the middle. Top with the shredded chicken and tomato salsa, then sprinkle over the chilli. Roll up the wraps, without folding in the sides.
3. Place on a baking tray, seam-side down, and bake for 15 minutes. Be careful when opening as the cheese will be gooey and hot. Cut in half and serve with rocket leaves.

TIP To make these vegetarian, omit the chicken and add strips of firm tofu instead.

1 SERVE =
½ UNIT PROTEIN
1 UNIT BREAD
1 UNIT VEGETABLES
2 UNITS FATS

Chicken and vegetable mountain bread wraps

SERVES 4 PREP TIME **15 minutes**

2 tablespoons pesto
2 tablespoons fat-free mayonnaise
1 teaspoon finely grated lemon zest
4 pieces low-GI mountain bread
1 small red capsicum (pepper), trimmed, seeded and cut into batons
1 Lebanese (small) cucumber, cut into batons
200 g cooked lean chicken breast, shredded
small handful basil leaves, shredded
60 g mixed lettuce leaves

A speedy choice for lunch. Cook some skinless chicken breast the night before and the rest is simple.

1 Combine the pesto, mayonnaise and lemon zest in a small bowl. Spread evenly over each piece of mountain bread.

2 Divide the capsicum and cucumber among the bread pieces, making a line starting about a third of the way across and leaving a 3 cm gap at the bottom. Top with chicken, basil and lettuce leaves. Season with freshly ground black pepper.

3 Fold the bottom third up, then gently roll up the bread to enclose the filling. Don't roll it too tightly or it may split. Slice on the diagonal and serve.

1 SERVE =
½ UNIT PROTEIN
1 UNIT BREAD
½ UNIT VEGETABLES
2¼ UNITS FATS

Mediterranean tuna toasts

SERVES 4 PREP TIME **10 minutes**
COOKING TIME **2 minutes**

- **200 g tinned tuna in spring water, drained**
- **½ small red onion, thinly sliced**
- **4 tablespoons pitted black olives, diced**
- **2 tablespoons drained capers, roughly chopped**
- **2 tablespoons fat-free mayonnaise**
- **4 slices low-GI wholemeal bread**
- **8 large crisp salad leaves, such as cos or radicchio**

The tuna mixture can be made in advance and refrigerated until needed.

1. Combine the tuna, onion, olives, capers and mayonnaise in a small bowl and season with freshly ground black pepper.
2. Toast the bread, then cut each slice in half diagonally to form two triangles. Place a lettuce leaf on each triangle, top with the tuna mixture and serve two triangles per person.

TIPS

This also makes a great sandwich filling. Spread two slices of bread with the tuna mixture and top with a lettuce leaf (remember, this will double the bread units).

These ingredients are delicious with pasta too. Cook 120 g wholemeal pasta, then toss in the tuna, onion, olives and capers and omit the mayonnaise. Replace the lettuce leaves with rocket.

Soups

1 SERVE =
1½ UNITS BREAD
1 UNIT VEGETABLES
1 UNIT FATS

Hearty barley and vegetable broth

SERVES 4 PREP TIME **15 minutes**
COOKING TIME **2 hours 15 minutes**

Barley is a nutritious, filling grain with a slightly nutty flavour. Unlike many other grains, it doesn't require pre-soaking.

1 tablespoon olive oil
1 large onion, chopped
1 leek, trimmed, white part only, washed and thinly sliced
1 large stick celery, quartered lengthways and chopped
2 cloves garlic, crushed
1 large carrot, diced
120 g pearl barley
1 bay leaf
1 sprig tarragon (optional)
1 litre salt-reduced vegetable stock or water
2 tablespoons chopped flat-leaf parsley

1 Heat the oil in a large heavy-based saucepan over medium heat. Add the onion, leek, celery and garlic and cook for 5 minutes, stirring regularly. Add the carrot and cook for a further 5 minutes.

2 Stir in the pearl barley, bay leaf, tarragon (if using) and vegetable stock or water. Bring to the boil, then reduce the heat to low and simmer, covered, for 1½–2 hours or until the barley is tender.

3 Remove the bay leaf and stir in the parsley. Season with freshly ground black pepper, if you like, and serve.

TIP To make a more substantial meal, add 200 g skinless chicken breast fillet for lunch (½ unit protein per serve) or 800 g skinless chicken breast fillet for dinner (2 protein units per serve).

1 SERVE =
2 UNITS BREAD
1 UNIT VEGETABLES
1 UNIT FATS

Red lentil and cannellini bean soup ›

SERVES 4 PREP TIME **10 minutes, plus soaking time**
COOKING TIME **2 hours 15 minutes**

You'll need to start this richly spiced soup the day before you wish to serve it, as the dried cannellini beans have to be soaked overnight. Dried cannellini beans are far healthier than tinned beans, which can have a fair amount of added sugar and salt. The lemon squeezed over at the end adds a delicious flavour, so don't be tempted to leave it out.

160 g dried cannellini beans, soaked overnight in cold water
1 tablespoon olive oil
1 large onion, chopped
2 cloves garlic, crushed
1 teaspoon ground cumin
1 teaspoon ground coriander
½ teaspoon chilli powder
¾ cup (150 g) split red lentils
1 × 400 g tin chopped tomatoes
1 litre salt-reduced vegetable stock or water
3 tablespoons chopped coriander (optional)
1 lemon, cut into wedges

1 Drain and rinse the cannellini beans, then set aside.

2 Heat the oil in a large heavy-based saucepan over medium heat. Add the onion and garlic and cook over low heat for 8–10 minutes without browning. Add the ground spices and cook, stirring, for 1 minute. Add the cannellini beans, lentils, tomatoes and stock or water and bring to the boil. Reduce the heat to very low and simmer gently for 1½–2 hours or until the beans are tender.

3 Stir in the coriander (if using) and serve with lemon wedges to squeeze over the soup.

1 SERVE =
½ UNIT BREAD
¼ UNIT DAIRY
1½ UNITS VEGETABLES
2 UNITS FATS

Roasted root vegetable soup

SERVES 4 PREP TIME **15 minutes** COOKING TIME **1 hour**

Celeriac is a very underrated vegetable. It has a delicious nutty flavour and makes a wonderful addition to winter soups. Don't buy an overly large one, though, as they can be tough.

2 tablespoons olive or canola oil
2 parsnips, peeled and cut into small chunks
1 small celeriac, peeled and cut into small chunks
2 carrots, cut into small chunks
1 onion, chopped
1 leek, trimmed, white part only, washed and roughly chopped
2 cloves garlic, chopped
1 litre salt-reduced vegetable stock or water
200 g reduced-fat Greek-style yoghurt

1 Preheat the oven to 180°C.

2 Pour 1 tablespoon of the oil into a baking dish and place in the oven. Once it is hot, add the parsnip, celeriac and carrot. Season with freshly ground black pepper and shake the pan around to coat the vegetables. Roast for 45 minutes.

3 Meanwhile, heat the remaining oil in a frying pan over low-medium heat and cook the onion, leek and garlic for 10 minutes. Add the stock or water. Cover and bring to the boil, then reduce the heat to low and simmer, covered, for 10 minutes. Add the roasted root vegetables and simmer for a further 10 minutes until tender. Cool for 5–10 minutes, then blend to a smooth puree.

4 Season with freshly ground black pepper and serve with a dollop of yoghurt.

1 SERVE =
1 UNIT PROTEIN
1 UNIT BREAD
1 UNIT VEGETABLES
1 UNIT FATS

Chilli chicken and black bean soup ›

SERVES 4 PREP TIME **15 minutes, plus soaking time**
COOKING TIME **2 hours 15 minutes**

Black beans are also known as turtle beans. They need to be soaked overnight, so start this recipe a day ahead.

¾ cup (150 g) black (turtle) beans, soaked overnight in cold water
1 tablespoon olive oil
1 onion, chopped
2 cloves garlic, crushed
1 red chilli, seeded and chopped, plus extra sliced chilli, to serve (optional)
1 red capsicum (pepper), trimmed, seeded and diced
1 sprig thyme
1 × 400 g tin chopped tomatoes
400 g skinless chicken breast fillet, thinly sliced
2 tablespoons chopped coriander

1 Soak the beans in water overnight. Drain and rinse, then set aside.

2 Heat the oil in a large saucepan over medium heat, then add the onion and garlic and cook for 5 minutes. Add the chilli, capsicum and thyme and cook for 5 minutes. Add the beans, tomatoes and 1.5 litres water and bring to the boil. Reduce the heat to very low and simmer very gently for 1¾ hours or until thick and the vegetables and beans are tender.

3 Add the chicken and cook for a further 15 minutes, or until the chicken is cooked through and the beans are soft. Season with freshly ground black pepper and scatter over the coriander and some extra chilli, if you like, before serving.

TIP Make this soup vegetarian by omitting the chicken and adding chopped carrots and celery with the capsicum.

1 SERVE =
1 UNIT PROTEIN
2 UNITS BREAD
2 UNITS VEGETABLES
½ UNIT FATS

Pork meatball, vegetable and noodle soup

SERVES 4 PREP TIME **25 minutes, plus soaking time**
COOKING TIME **10 minutes**

80 g bean-thread vermicelli noodles
400 g lean minced pork
3 spring onions, finely chopped
3 teaspoons finely grated ginger
1 clove garlic, crushed
1 litre salt-reduced chicken stock
2 teaspoons canola or vegetable oil
200 g shiitake mushrooms, thinly sliced
120 g snowpeas (mange-tout), sliced on the diagonal
230 g baby corn, cut into 2 cm pieces
2 tablespoons salt-reduced soy sauce
1 teaspoon Chinese black vinegar (optional)

This is a delicate, broth-style soup.

1 Soak the noodles in hot water for 5 minutes to soften (or according to the packet instructions). Drain, then set aside.

2 Combine the pork mince, spring onion, ginger and garlic and season with freshly ground black pepper. Wet your hands slightly and form the mixture into about twenty-four small meatballs, about 1–2 cm in diameter. Set aside.

3 Bring the stock to the boil, then reduce to a simmer.

4 Heat the oil in a large saucepan over medium heat. Add the mushrooms and stir-fry for 3 minutes. Add the snowpeas and baby corn and stir to combine. Pour in the hot stock and return to the boil. Add the meatballs and simmer for 4–5 minutes or until cooked through. Stir in the soy sauce and black vinegar (if using).

5 To serve, divide the noodles among four bowls, then ladle over the soup and meatballs.

TIPS

If you like your soup spicy, add some finely chopped red chilli when you add the stock, or add an extra teaspoon of finely grated ginger when you fry the mushrooms.

You could also scatter some trimmed bean sprouts over the soup just before serving, and accompany with lemon wedges for squeezing over.

1 SERVE =
1 UNIT PROTEIN
1 UNIT VEGETABLES

Asian prawn and vegetable broth

SERVES 4 PREP TIME **30 minutes, plus marinating time**
COOKING TIME **25 minutes**

1 tablespoon fish sauce
½–1 small red chilli, seeded and finely chopped
1 tablespoon lime juice
400 g raw peeled prawns, with tails intact
1 litre salt-reduced vegetable stock
200 ml boiling water
1 stalk lemongrass, cut into four pieces, bruised
4 kaffir lime leaves, torn
4 thin slices ginger
1 large zucchini (courgette), halved lengthways, then cut into 2 cm lengths
1 bunch asparagus, trimmed and cut into 5 mm rounds

TO SERVE
80 g bean sprouts, trimmed
small handful coriander leaves
chilli sauce or chilli flakes
lemon wedges

This light, fragrant broth is ideal for a summer's evening, but it's also good on a winter's night when the chilli will warm you up. Buy 400 g ready-peeled prawns from the supermarket to save time.

1 Combine the fish sauce, chilli and lime juice in a bowl. Add the prawns and toss to coat, then set aside for 15 minutes while you prepare the soup.

2 Pour the stock and the boiling water into a large saucepan, then add the lemongrass, lime leaves and ginger. Bring to the boil, then reduce the heat and simmer, covered, for 15 minutes. Scoop out the flavourings and discard.

3 Return the broth to the boil, add the zucchini and asparagus and cook for 1 minute. Add the prawns and marinade and cook for 2–3 minutes or until the prawns are pink and cooked through.

4 Serve topped with the bean sprouts and coriander leaves, with the chilli and lemon wedges on the side.

TIPS

You could easily make this soup using chicken instead. Simply replace the prawns with 400 g sliced skinless chicken breast fillet. Cook for 5–10 minutes or until the chicken is cooked through, adding the zucchini and asparagus for the final 4–5 minutes of cooking.

Serve this with regular chilli sauce, rather than sweet chilli sauce – the latter is loaded with sugar.

1 SERVE =
1 UNIT PROTEIN
1 UNIT BREAD
1½ UNITS VEGETABLES
1 UNIT FATS

Roasted tomato and capsicum soup with prawns and garlic croutons

SERVES 4 PREP TIME **30 minutes, plus standing time**
COOKING TIME **1 hour 10 minutes**

2 large red capsicums (peppers)
2 cloves garlic, crushed
1 tablespoon olive oil
6 tomatoes, halved lengthways
1 red onion, roughly chopped
1 leek, trimmed, white part only, washed and thinly sliced
1 sprig thyme, plus extra leaves to serve (optional)
400 g raw peeled prawns, with tails intact
½ lemon

GARLIC CROUTONS

2 day-old wholegrain low-GI bread rolls, thickly sliced
1 large clove garlic, halved

There are a few steps involved in making this soup, but they are all simple. It can be cooked in advance and reheated when needed, but don't cook the prawns or garlic croutons until just before serving. Buy 400 g ready-peeled prawns from the supermarket to save time.

1 Preheat the oven grill to high and line the grill tray with foil.

2 Place the capsicums under the griller for 15–20 minutes until the skin blackens, turning regularly so that all the skin is charred. Don't worry – the capsicums won't burn. Put them straight into a plastic bag, seal it well and set aside for 20 minutes. Peel or rub off the skins, but don't wash under running water or you will lose much of the flavour. Remove the seeds and roughly chop the flesh, saving any juices if possible.

3 Meanwhile, preheat the oven to 170°C.

4 Combine the garlic and 2 teaspoons of the oil and season well with freshly ground black pepper. Brush the cut sides of the tomatoes with the garlic oil. Place on a baking tray, cut-side up, and roast for 30 minutes or until softened and slightly blackened. Remove the skins, if you like.

5 Heat 1 teaspoon oil in a large saucepan over medium heat. Add the onion, leek and thyme and cook, covered, for 8 minutes or until softened. Add the capsicum, tomato halves and about 3 cups (750 ml) water. Bring to the boil, then reduce the heat and simmer for 5 minutes. Set aside to cool for 10 minutes. Remove the thyme sprig, then puree the soup until smooth. Reheat gently.

6 To make the garlic croutons, toast the bread, then rub all over with the cut sides of the garlic clove. Break into bite-sized pieces.

7 Just before serving, heat the remaining oil in a frying pan. Add the prawns and stir-fry for 2–3 minutes or until pink and cooked through. Squeeze over the lemon juice and toss the prawns to coat.

8 Divide the soup among four bowls, then top with a quarter of the prawns, season with freshly ground black pepper and sprinkle with extra thyme, if you like. Serve with the garlic croutons.

1 SERVE =
1 UNIT PROTEIN
½ UNIT BREAD
½ UNIT DAIRY
½ UNIT VEGETABLES

Chicken and baby corn soup

SERVES 4 PREP TIME **10 minutes** COOKING TIME **30 minutes**

1 litre salt-reduced chicken stock
1 cup (250 ml) reduced-fat coconut-flavoured evaporated milk
4 kaffir lime leaves
1 stalk lemongrass, halved and bruised
½–1 small red chilli, thinly sliced (optional)
1–2 tablespoons fish sauce
400 g skinless chicken breast fillet, thinly sliced
115 g baby corn, sliced on the diagonal
small handful coriander leaves

This soup can be as mild or spicy as you like, depending on how much chilli you add. You can leave it out completely if you like – the soup is just as delicious without it.

1 Place the chicken stock, evaporated milk, lime leaves, lemongrass and chilli in a large heavy-based saucepan and bring to the boil. Reduce the heat to low and simmer, covered, for 20 minutes to allow the flavours to infuse. Remove and discard the lime leaves and lemongrass, if you like.
2 Increase the heat to high, add the fish sauce and chicken and cook for 3 minutes. Add the baby corn and cook for a further 3–4 minutes or until the chicken is cooked through. Taste and add a little extra fish sauce, if necessary.
3 Spoon into four bowls, scatter over the coriander leaves and serve.

TIPS

You can add additional vegetables, such as sliced snowpeas (mange-tout), asparagus or small pieces of broccolini at the same time as the baby corn.

To make this soup vegetarian, use vegetable stock or water instead of chicken stock and omit the chicken and fish sauce. Throw in plenty of sliced fresh vegetables.

Don't be tempted to add lime juice, as people sometimes do with Asian soups, as it will cause the evaporated milk to curdle.

1 SERVE =
1 UNIT BREAD
1 UNIT VEGETABLES
½ UNIT FATS

Green pea soup

SERVES 4 PREP TIME **25 minutes, plus soaking and cooling time**
COOKING TIME **1 hour 50 minutes**

140 g green split peas
2 teaspoons canola or olive oil
1 large onion, roughly chopped
1 clove garlic, crushed
2 carrots, roughly chopped
2 sticks celery, roughly chopped
1½ teaspoons ground cumin
1 teaspoon ground coriander
1 teaspoon curry powder
1 litre salt-reduced vegetable stock or water
1 cup (250 ml) boiling water
100 g frozen peas
large handful flat-leaf parsley, roughly chopped

Green split peas have quite a sweet flavour and are excellent in winter soups. They are a rich source of fibre, which helps to maintain blood glucose levels and lower blood cholesterol. Soaking the split peas for a couple of hours before cooking makes them easier to digest.

1. Soak the peas in cold water for 2 hours. Drain, then rinse and drain again.
2. Heat the oil in a large saucepan over medium heat. Add the onion and garlic and cook for 5 minutes, stirring regularly. Add the carrot and celery and cook for 5 minutes. Stir in the cumin, coriander and curry powder and cook for 1–2 minutes.
3. Add the split peas, stock or water and the boiling water. Bring to the boil, then reduce the heat to low and simmer, covered, for 1½ hours or until the peas are tender. Stir in the frozen peas and cook for 2 minutes, then set aside to cool for 5 minutes.
4. Roughly chop about 1 tablespoon of the parsley and set aside. Add the remaining parsley to the soup and puree until smooth.
5. Gently reheat the soup, then spoon into bowls and serve with the chopped parsley scattered over the top.

TIP Combining the green split peas with frozen peas and parsley dramatically increases the amount of iron your body will absorb from the peas, due to the vitamin C in the peas and parsley.

1 SERVE =
½ UNIT BREAD
2 UNITS VEGETABLES
2 UNITS FATS

Gazpacho with pesto croutons

SERVES 4 PREP TIME **45 minutes, plus refrigerating time**
COOKING TIME **3 minutes**

2 ice cubes
8 firm, ripe tomatoes
1 green capsicum (pepper), trimmed, seeded and finely diced
1 clove garlic, crushed
200 ml tomato juice
2 tablespoons sherry vinegar or red wine vinegar
1 tablespoon extra virgin olive oil
½ red onion, finely chopped
½ Lebanese (small) cucumber, finely chopped

PESTO CROUTONS
2 slices day-old wholegrain low-GI bread
1 tablespoon pesto

Tomatoes are packed full of lycopene, the antioxidant important in helping prevent heart disease and some cancers. They are also a great source of potassium and vitamins C and E. This chilled soup is the perfect way to enjoy them on a hot summer's day.

1 Put the ice cubes in a jug with 300 ml cold water and refrigerate.

2 Cut a shallow cross into the base of each tomato. Working in batches, place tomatoes in a bowl of boiling water for 30 seconds, then plunge into cold water for 10 seconds. Remove and peel, starting from the cross.

3 Place a sieve over a bowl. Quarter the tomatoes and scoop out the seeds into the sieve. Finely dice the tomato flesh and place in a bowl with the capsicum and garlic. Stir to combine. Squeeze the juice from the seeds and add to the bowl, discarding the seeds. Stir in the tomato juice, vinegar and oil and mix well, then cover and refrigerate for at least 2 hours.

4 Meanwhile, to make the croutons, brush the bread with the pesto on one side, then cut into small squares. Fry in a dry frying pan over medium–high heat for 2–3 minutes or until crunchy. Transfer to a small serving bowl.

5 Place the red onion and cucumber in two small bowls.

6 Just before serving, add enough of the reserved iced water to thin the soup slightly. Serve with the croutons and the onion and cucumber garnishes.

TIPS

It's vital to use ripe, full-flavoured tomatoes for this soup; pale orange ones simply won't do.

This soup will happily sit for up to 12 hours in the fridge, so it's a good dish to prepare ahead of time.

1 SERVE =
¼ UNIT PROTEIN
1 UNIT BREAD
¼ UNIT DAIRY
½ UNIT VEGETABLES
1 UNIT FATS

Pumpkin, bacon and coconut soup

SERVES 4 PREP TIME **20 minutes, plus cooling time**
COOKING TIME **45 minutes**

1 tablespoon canola or olive oil
500 g pumpkin (squash) flesh, roughly chopped into 2–3 cm pieces
2 teaspoons ground cumin
1 teaspoon ground coriander
2 rashers lean, rindless bacon, trimmed of all fat
1 onion, roughly chopped
2 cloves garlic, crushed
1 cup (250 ml) reduced-fat coconut-flavoured evaporated milk
1 tablespoon snipped chives or chopped coriander

Although delicious as a meal in itself, you could serve this soup with some low-GI wholemeal toast to make it more substantial. If you don't have a stick blender, puree it in a food processor or blender.

1 Preheat the oven to 180°C.

2 Pour 2 teaspoons oil into a baking tray and place it in the oven. Once it is hot, add the pumpkin, cumin and coriander and shake the pan around so the pumpkin is well coated in the oil and spices. Roast for 30–40 minutes or until the pumpkin is soft – the cooking time will vary depending on the type of pumpkin you use.

3 Meanwhile, heat the remaining oil in a saucepan over high heat. Add the bacon and fry for 2–3 minutes or until just crisp. Remove, leaving any oil in the pan, and dice. Set aside.

4 Add the onion and garlic to the pan and cook over low-medium heat for 6–8 minutes. Add the evaporated milk and 1¾ cups (430 ml) water and bring to the boil. Add the roasted pumpkin, then reduce the heat and simmer, covered, for 5 minutes. Leave to cool for 5 minutes, then puree.

5 Gently reheat the soup, then serve garnished with the bacon bits and a scattering of chives or coriander.

TIP To add a bit of heat to this dish, try adding a teaspoon of harissa paste or a couple of teaspoons of red or green curry paste when frying the onions.

Substantial salads

1 SERVE =
2 UNITS PROTEIN
2 UNITS VEGETABLES
2 UNITS FATS

Lemongrass beef salad

SERVES 4 PREP TIME **20 minutes, plus marinating time**
COOKING TIME **10 minutes**

1 tablespoon lime juice
1½ tablespoons olive oil
1 small red onion, halved and thinly sliced
small handful mint leaves, larger leaves torn
small handful coriander leaves
100 g mixed salad leaves
1 × 250 g punnet cherry tomatoes, halved
2 Lebanese (small) cucumbers, halved lengthways, then sliced on the diagonal

LEMONGRASS BEEF
2 stalks lemongrass, white part only, finely chopped
2 cloves garlic, crushed
½–1 small red chilli, seeded and finely chopped
2 teaspoons olive oil
1 tablespoon lime juice
1 tablespoon fish sauce
800 g beef rump or sirloin steak
cooking oil spray

If you can, start this recipe a day ahead so the beef can marinate overnight. And take care not to cook it for too long – the beef rests for 10 minutes after cooking and it will continue to cook during this time.

1. To prepare the lemongrass beef, pound the lemongrass, garlic, chilli and some freshly ground black pepper in a mortar and pestle for 2 minutes. Stir in the oil, lime juice and fish sauce. Place the beef in a shallow dish, spoon over the marinade, then rub it into the beef, ensuring it is well coated. Cover and marinate in the fridge for at least 2 hours and up to 24 hours.
2. Preheat a chargrill pan or frying pan over medium heat. Pat the beef dry, then spray lightly with cooking oil. Cook the beef for 4–5 minutes each side for medium–rare or until cooked to your liking. The length of time will depend on the thickness of the beef. Remove and cover with foil, then leave to rest for 10 minutes.
3. Meanwhile, whisk together the lime juice and oil. Combine the remaining salad ingredients in a large bowl. Add the dressing and toss well.
4. Slice the beef and either toss it through the salad or serve on top.

TIP This is a great salad to enjoy for dinner, but if you want to have it for lunch, reduce the quantity of beef to 200 g (which reduces the protein count to ½ unit per serve).

1 SERVE =
1 UNIT PROTEIN
¼ UNIT DAIRY
½ UNIT VEGETABLES
1 UNIT FATS

Poached chicken and watercress salad with yoghurt dressing

SERVES 4 PREP TIME **25 minutes, plus marinating and cooling time**
COOKING TIME **10 minutes**

½ bunch watercress, thick stalks discarded
2 Lebanese (small) cucumbers, halved lengthways and thickly sliced
⅔ cup (80 g) pitted black olives, chopped
200 g reduced-fat Greek-style yoghurt
2 spring onions, finely chopped

POACHED CHICKEN
400 g skinless chicken breast fillet
3 tablespoons lemon juice
small bunch thyme
1 bay leaf
5 black peppercorns
6 juniper berries, crushed
2 teaspoons cider vinegar

The dressing for this salad uses a little of the delicious poaching liquid for added flavour. You could use rocket instead of watercress, if you prefer.

1 To prepare the poached chicken, cut the chicken breasts in half widthways through the centre to form thin slices so they will cook more quickly. Place in a ziplock bag. Combine the remaining poaching ingredients and pour over the chicken, then seal the bag and leave to marinate in the fridge for 2 hours.

2 Open the bag and tip the chicken and marinade into a saucepan with just enough water to cover the chicken. Bring slowly to the boil, then reduce the heat and simmer, covered, for 8 minutes, turning the chicken once during poaching. Leave to cool in the water for 20 minutes. Remove the chicken from the poaching liquid and shred into small pieces. Strain the liquid and reserve it for later.

3 Meanwhile, combine the watercress, cucumber and olives in a bowl. Toss through the shredded chicken and divide among serving glasses or bowls.

4 To make the dressing, whisk together the yoghurt, spring onion and 4 tablespoons of the poaching liquid. Pour the dressing over the warm chicken salad. Serve with any leftover dressing to the side.

1 SERVE =
2 UNITS PROTEIN
1½ UNITS VEGETABLES
1½ UNITS FATS

6/10

Prawn and fennel salad

SERVES 4 PREP TIME **15 minutes, plus refrigerating time**
COOKING TIME **8 minutes**

800 g raw peeled prawns, with tails intact
20 g flaked almonds
1 large bulb fennel, trimmed, feathery fronds reserved
1 baby cos lettuce, shredded
1 Lebanese (small) cucumber, thinly sliced or diced

DRESSING
20 g fat-free mayonnaise
1 tablespoon lemon juice
2 teaspoons olive oil
1½ tablespoons finely chopped mint

For speed, you could buy cooked, peeled prawns; however, the flavour and texture will be far superior if you cook raw prawns and dress them while still warm. If you're having this salad for lunch, reduce the quantity of peeled prawns to 200 g (½ protein unit).

1 To make the dressing, combine all the ingredients in a small bowl, adding 1 tablespoon warm water and 1 tablespoon of the finely chopped reserved fennel fronds. Set aside.

2 Cook the prawns in two batches in a large saucepan of simmering water for 2–3 minutes or until pink and just cooked through. Drain well and pat dry. Place in a large bowl and, while still warm, pour over the dressing and toss to combine. Cover and cool in the fridge for 20 minutes. If using pre-cooked prawns, simply toss them in the dressing and chill for 20 minutes.

3 Heat a small frying pan over medium heat. Add the almonds and toast for 1–2 minutes until light golden, shaking the pan regularly. Set aside.

4 Slice the fennel bulb in half top to bottom and remove the core. Place the fennel on a board, cut-side down, and thinly slice. Combine with the lettuce leaves and cucumber and place on a serving dish. Top with the prawns and scatter over the toasted almonds, then garnish with any remaining fennel fronds and serve.

TIP If chilling this salad before serving, remove it from the fridge at least 20 minutes before you want to eat it to bring it to room temperature. This will make it more flavoursome.

1 SERVE =
½ UNIT PROTEIN
2 UNITS BREAD
1½ UNITS VEGETABLES
2 UNITS FATS

Brown rice salad with chicken, broccoli and chilli dressing

SERVES 4 PREP TIME **20 minutes, plus standing time**
COOKING TIME **6 minutes**

2 teaspoons sesame seeds
150 g broccoli, cut into small florets
360 g cooked brown rice (from 160 g uncooked)
200 g cooked skinless chicken breast, shredded
1 red capsicum (pepper), trimmed, seeded and cut into strips
1 yellow capsicum (pepper), trimmed, seeded and cut into strips
20 g pistachios, roughly chopped

CHILLI DRESSING
½ small red chilli, seeded and finely chopped
1 clove garlic, crushed
2 red or golden shallots, finely chopped
1 tablespoon fish sauce
1 tablespoon mirin
3 teaspoons olive oil
1 tablespoon lemon juice

This salad can be prepared a day ahead, then taken for a packed lunch, or simply enjoy it at home for lunch. You can use leftover cooked brown rice, otherwise get the rice cooking as soon as you start the recipe.

1 To make the dressing, whisk together all the ingredients and set aside to allow the flavours to develop.
2 Heat a small frying pan over medium heat and toast the sesame seeds for 1–2 minutes or until golden, shaking the pan regularly. Transfer to a small bowl and set aside.
3 Steam the broccoli florets for 3–4 minutes or until tender. Rinse under cold water until cool, then drain well.
4 Combine the rice, chicken, capsicum, sesame seeds and broccoli and toss gently to combine. Pour over the dressing and toss to coat, then scatter over the pistachios. Set aside for 30 minutes before serving (put it in the fridge if it's a hot day).

1 SERVE =
1 UNIT BREAD
1½ UNITS VEGETABLES
1 UNIT FATS

Roast zucchini salad with lemon and herb dressing

SERVES 4 PREP TIME **15 minutes** COOKING TIME **30 minutes**

2 teaspoons olive oil
2 zucchinis (courgettes), cut into 1 cm slices
1 teaspoon ground cumin
300 g green beans, trimmed and cut into 3 cm lengths
1 × 400 g tin borlotti beans, rinsed and drained
1 bunch radishes, trimmed and diced

LEMON AND HERB DRESSING
2 tablespoons chopped mint
1 tablespoon snipped chives
1 tablespoon lemon juice
2 teaspoons olive oil

Serve this filling salad as an accompaniment to grilled fish or lean chicken or increase the borlotti beans to 600 g to provide a protein unit.

1. Preheat the oven to 180°C.
2. Pour the oil into a baking dish and place in the oven. Once the oil is hot, add the zucchini and cumin. Season with freshly ground black pepper and toss so the zucchini is well coated in the oil and spices. Roast for 30 minutes, shaking the dish occasionally.
3. Meanwhile, blanch the green beans in boiling water for 3 minutes or until just tender. Drain, then refresh in a bowl of cold water. Drain well and place in a serving bowl with the borlotti beans and radish, then mix together well. Set aside.
4. To make the dressing, whisk together all the ingredients.
5. Pour the dressing over the salad and toss to combine. Add the roasted zucchini and toss again. Serve straight away or chill in the fridge until needed.

1 SERVE =
1 UNIT PROTEIN
1½ UNITS VEGETABLES
2 UNITS FATS

Cannellini and green bean salad with Italian dressing

SERVES 4 PREP TIME **30 minutes, plus soaking time**
COOKING TIME **1 hour 30 minutes**

1½ cups (300 g) cannellini beans, soaked overnight in cold water
4 eggs
300 g green beans, trimmed and cut into 3 cm lengths
1 small red onion, halved and thinly sliced
1 × 250 g punnet cherry tomatoes, halved
50 g rocket leaves, roughly torn
80 g small black olives (Ligurian olives)
small handful basil leaves, torn if large

ITALIAN DRESSING
1½ tablespoons olive oil
1 tablespoon balsamic vinegar
2 teaspoons wholegrain mustard
2 tablespoons shredded basil leaves

The cannellini beans need to be soaked overnight, so start this recipe the day before. You could use a 400 g tin of drained and rinsed cannellini beans if you're pushed for time, but cooking your own is healthier.

1 Drain and rinse the cannellini beans well, then place in a saucepan and cover with about 10 cm water. Bring to the boil, then reduce the heat to low and simmer, covered, for 1–1½ hours or until the beans are tender but not too soft. Drain and set aside.

2 Meanwhile, cook the eggs in simmering water for 7 minutes. Drain, then refresh in a bowl of cold water. Peel and cut into quarters.

3 Blanch the green beans in boiling water for 3 minutes or until just tender. Drain, then refresh in a bowl of cold water. Drain well and place in a serving bowl with the onion, tomatoes, rocket, olives and basil.

4 To make the dressing, whisk together all the ingredients and season with freshly ground black pepper.

5 Add the cooked cannellini beans to the salad, drizzle over the dressing and toss to combine. Top with the eggs and serve (reminding your guests that the olives have stones).

1 SERVE =
2 UNITS PROTEIN
1 UNIT BREAD
¼ UNIT DAIRY
1 UNIT VEGETABLES

Rice salad with salmon and herbs

SERVES 4 PREP TIME **25 minutes, plus cooling time**
COOKING TIME **40 minutes**

20 g wild rice
60 g basmati rice
800 g salmon fillet, skin removed and pin-boned
1 bunch asparagus, trimmed and cut into 2 cm pieces
2 teaspoons drained capers, rinsed and chopped
handful flat-leaf parsley leaves, roughly chopped
1 small handful mint leaves
1 small head radicchio
50 g watercress, tough stalks discarded, or rocket leaves
200 g reduced-fat Greek-style yoghurt
2 tablespoons lime juice

Wild rice is not actually a rice but a native American grass. It adds a good chewy texture to rice salad. If you want to serve this salad for lunch, reduce the salmon to 200 g (and your protein count to ½ unit).

1. Cook the wild rice and basmati rice according to the packet instructions. Drain well, then combine and set aside.
2. Preheat the oven grill to high and line the grill tray with foil. Cut the salmon into four long pieces, then cook under the grill for 2–3 minutes each side or until just cooked through. Cool for 5 minutes, then break into bite-sized chunks.
3. Meanwhile, blanch the asparagus in boiling water for 2 minutes or until just cooked. Drain, then refresh in a bowl of cold water. Drain well and add to the rice, along with the capers, parsley and mint and gently toss to combine.
4. Discard any tough outer leaves from the radicchio, then halve lengthways. Remove the core, then shred widthways. Add to the salad with the salmon and watercress or rocket and gently toss again.
5. Combine the yoghurt and lime juice and season with freshly ground black pepper. Spoon over the salad and serve with any leftover dressing to the side.

TIP This dish is best served while the salmon is still warm or at room temperature. If you are making it in advance and chilling is required, bring the salad to room temperature before serving.

1 SERVE =
¼ UNIT DAIRY
¼ UNIT FRUIT
2 UNITS VEGETABLES
1½ UNITS FATS

Roasted beetroot and cauliflower salad with tahini dressing

SERVES 4 PREP TIME **20 minutes, plus cooling time**
COOKING TIME **1 hour 30 minutes**

450–500 g beetroot
300 g cauliflower, broken into small florets
2 teaspoons olive oil
½ cup (40 g) flaked almonds
60 g wild rocket
1 small red onion, halved and thinly sliced
40 g raisins

TAHINI DRESSING
1 tablespoon tahini
1½ tablespoons lemon juice
200 g reduced-fat Greek-style yoghurt

The traditional Middle Eastern-inspired flavours of this salad may seem a little unusual, but be adventurous as it is well worth trying. This is wonderful as a side salad with grilled meat or fish.

1. Preheat the oven to 180°C.
2. Trim the tops and bottoms of the beetroot, then scrub but do not peel. Wrap in foil and bake for 1–1¼ hours or until a skewer goes easily into the beetroot. Cool for 10 minutes, then rub off the skins (wearing rubber gloves, to prevent purple-stained hands). Cut into bite-sized chunks.
3. Meanwhile, blanch the cauliflower florets for 5 minutes, then drain well.
4. Place the cauliflower and beetroot in a baking dish, drizzle over the oil and roast for 15 minutes.
5. To make the tahini dressing, combine all the ingredients in a small bowl, adding 2 teaspoons water.
6. Heat a small frying pan over medium heat. Add the almonds and toast for 1–2 minutes until golden, shaking the pan regularly. Remove from the pan and set aside.
7. Combine the rocket and onion in a serving bowl and top with the beetroot and cauliflower. Spoon over the dressing and finish with a scattering of flaked almonds and raisins. Serve.

1 SERVE =
½ UNIT PROTEIN
2 UNITS BREAD
1 UNIT VEGETABLES
1 UNIT FATS

Couscous salad with shredded chicken and roasted vegetables

SERVES 4 PREP TIME **30 minutes** COOKING TIME **40 minutes**

1 tablespoon olive oil
1 red capsicum (pepper), trimmed, seeded and cut into 1–2 cm pieces
1 yellow capsicum (pepper), trimmed, seeded and cut into 1–2 cm pieces
2 zucchinis (courgettes), halved lengthways and cut into 1 cm slices
1 red onion, cut into thin wedges
160 g couscous
2–3 tablespoons lemon juice, as needed
3 tablespoons roughly chopped flat-leaf parsley
1 tablespoon snipped chives
200 g cooked skinless chicken breast, shredded

If you can't find yellow capsicum, just use two red ones. This salad can be made several hours in advance, covered and chilled in the fridge until needed.

1 Preheat the oven to 180°C.

2 Pour 2 teaspoons of the oil into a baking dish and place in the oven. Once the oil is hot, add the capsicum, zucchini and onion. Season with freshly ground black pepper and toss so the vegetables are well coated in the oil and pepper. Roast for 40 minutes or until tender, shaking the dish occasionally. Set the vegetables aside to cool to room temperature.

3 Meanwhile, bring 1 cup (250 ml) water to the boil in a small saucepan. Add the couscous and fork through the grains to separate them. Remove the pan from the heat, cover and leave to stand for 2 minutes. Return the pan to a very low heat and cook for 3 minutes, continuing to fork through the grains. Remove the pan from the heat and stir the grains gently. Add the lemon juice to taste, parsley, chives and remaining oil, season well with freshly ground black pepper and set aside for 10 minutes.

4 Stir the chicken and cooled roasted vegetables into the couscous and serve.

1 SERVE =
2 UNITS PROTEIN
1 UNIT BREAD
2½ UNITS VEGETABLES
2 UNITS FATS

Fresh tuna nicoise salad

SERVES 4 PREP TIME **35 minutes** COOKING TIME **35 minutes**

400 g chat potatoes
4 eggs
250 g green beans, trimmed and halved
3 firm, ripe tomatoes, roughly chopped
80 g pitted kalamata olives
olive oil, for brushing
700 g tuna steaks (or 700 g tinned tuna in spring water, drained)
1 baby cos lettuce, leaves roughly torn

DRESSING
1½ tablespoons olive oil
1 tablespoon red wine vinegar
1 teaspoon Dijon mustard
1 small clove garlic, crushed
2 teaspoons finely chopped thyme (or 1 teaspoon dried thyme)

This is a delicious option for dinner on a summer's evening. You can try it for lunch too – just reduce the tuna to 400 g (100 g per serve).

1 Place the potatoes in a saucepan of cold water. Bring to the boil, then reduce the heat and simmer for 15–20 minutes until tender. Drain. When cool enough to handle, cut into thick slices and place in a bowl.

2 Meanwhile, cook the eggs in simmering water for 7 minutes. Drain, then refresh in cold water. Peel and cut into quarters.

3 Blanch the beans in simmering water for 3 minutes or until just tender. Drain, then refresh in cold water and drain well. Add to the potatoes, along with the tomatoes and olives.

4 If using fresh tuna, preheat a chargrill pan over medium heat. Brush the tuna lightly with oil and chargrill for 4–5 minutes each side or until just cooked through; the cooking time will depend on the thickness of the fish. Set aside for 5 minutes, then slice.

5 To make the dressing, whisk together all the ingredients and season with freshly ground black pepper. Pour most of it over the potato mixture and toss gently to combine.

6 Arrange the cos lettuce in a shallow serving dish. Add the potato mixture, then top with the eggs and tuna. Drizzle over the remaining dressing and serve.

TIP All the elements for this salad can be prepared ahead of time, and you can dress the potato mixture in advance too. Wait until the last minute, though, to bring it all together, otherwise the lettuce leaves may go soggy.

1 SERVE =
½ UNIT PROTEIN
1 UNIT BREAD
2 UNITS VEGETABLES
2 UNITS FATS

Chickpea salad with roasted vegetables, tuna and tomatoes

SERVES 4 PREP TIME **20 minutes** COOKING TIME **30 minutes**

2 teaspoons olive oil
2 red capsicums (peppers), trimmed, seeded and cut into 3 cm pieces
2 zucchinis (courgettes), halved lengthways and cut into 2 cm pieces
1 × 250 g punnet cherry tomatoes
1 × 400 g tin chickpeas, rinsed and drained
3 tablespoons pitted kalamata olives, halved
200 g tinned tuna in spring water, drained
2 teaspoons oregano leaves, plus extra to garnish
3 teaspoons olive oil
2 tablespoons white wine vinegar

Roasting vegetables really brings out their flavour, and the tuna rounds out the salad beautifully. If you're eating this for dinner, add another 200 g tuna for 1 unit protein per serve.

1 Preheat the oven to 180°C.

2 Pour the oil into a baking dish and place in the oven. Once the oil is hot, add the capsicum, zucchini and tomatoes. Season with freshly ground black pepper and toss so the vegetables are well coated in the oil and pepper. Roast for 30 minutes or until the vegetables are tender, shaking the dish occasionally. Set the vegetables aside to cool to room temperature.

3 Place the chickpeas, olives and tuna in a large bowl and toss gently.

4 Combine the oregano, oil and vinegar and season with freshly ground black pepper. Drizzle over the salad and toss to combine. Set aside.

5 Add the cooled roasted vegetables to the salad, then garnish with extra oregano leaves and serve.

1 SERVE =
½ UNIT PROTEIN
2 UNITS BREAD
2 UNITS VEGETABLES
½ UNIT FATS

Marinated tofu salad with soba noodles

SERVES 4 PREP TIME **25 minutes, plus marinating and refrigerating time**
COOKING TIME **10 minutes**

2 teaspoons white miso paste
2 tablespoons salt-reduced soy sauce
1 tablespoon rice wine vinegar
2 tablespoons mirin
1 teaspoon sesame oil
1 clove garlic, crushed
2 teaspoons finely grated ginger
250 g firm tofu
160 g soba noodles
150 g snowpeas (mange-tout), trimmed
80 g snowpea (mange-tout) sprouts, halved
50 g mizuna leaves, roughly torn
3 spring onions, thinly sliced on the diagonal

This delicious lunch combines many popular Japanese ingredients, such as miso, mizuna and soba noodles, which are now widely available from larger supermarkets or Asian food stores.

1 Place the miso paste and 2 tablespoons hot water in a small bowl and set aside until the miso has dissolved. Stir to combine, then add the soy sauce, vinegar, mirin, sesame oil, garlic and ginger.

2 Carefully cut the tofu into 2 cm cubes and place in a shallow heatproof dish that will fit in a steamer basket or large sieve. Pour the marinade evenly over the tofu and set aside for 30 minutes.

3 Cook the soba noodles in boiling water for 4 minutes or according to the packet instructions. Drain, return to the pan and pour cold water over them. Leave for 2 minutes to cool down, then drain again and place in a large bowl with the snowpeas, sprouts and mizuna leaves.

4 Gently turn the cubes of tofu to coat in the marinade, then steam for 5 minutes or until warm through over simmering water. If using a sieve, sit the sieve over a saucepan of simmering water and cover with the lid.

5 Carefully remove the dish from the steamer and set aside to cool for 5 minutes. Transfer the tofu to a small bowl, leaving the marinade, then place both the tofu and the marinade in the fridge to chill for 20 minutes.

6 Pour enough of the marinade over the noodle mixture to moisten it well, then gently sit the tofu on top. Scatter over the spring onion and serve with any remaining marinade to the side.

TIP Mizuna leaves are spiky green leaves used in salads and hot pots in Japanese cuisine. If you can't find them, use rocket leaves instead.

1 SERVE =
2 UNITS PROTEIN
1 UNIT BREAD
2 UNITS VEGETABLES
2½ UNITS FATS

Rack of lamb with couscous salad

SERVES 4 PREP TIME **30 minutes, plus resting time**
COOKING TIME **15 minutes**

2 × 400 g lamb racks with four cutlets each
1 teaspoon finely grated lemon zest
4 tablespoons finely chopped flat-leaf parsley
1 tablespoon olive oil
80 g couscous
2 tablespoons lemon juice
3 tablespoons chopped mint
3 tablespoons pitted kalamata olives, chopped
1 bunch asparagus, trimmed and cut into 1 cm lengths
1 × 250 g punnet cherry tomatoes, quartered
20 g pistachios, chopped
20 g almonds, chopped

This salad, featuring tender lamb, fresh herbs and nuts, makes for an impressive dinner. The couscous can be prepared earlier in the day and refrigerated until you're ready to serve.

1 Preheat the oven to 200°C.

2 Trim any fat from the lamb racks and wrap the bones in foil to prevent them burning. Combine the lemon zest, 1 tablespoon of the parsley and 2 teaspoons of the oil and season well with freshly ground black pepper. Rub all over the meaty side of the lamb. Place in a small roasting tin and cook for 15 minutes for medium-rare or until cooked to your liking, then cover with foil and set aside to rest for 10 minutes.

3 Meanwhile, bring ½ cup (125 ml) water to the boil in a small saucepan. Add the couscous and fork through the grains to separate them. Remove the pan from the heat, then cover and leave to stand for 2 minutes. Return the pan to a very low heat and cook for 3 minutes, continuing to fork through the grains. Remove the pan from the heat and stir the grains gently. Add the lemon juice, mint, olives, remaining oil and remaining parsley. Season with freshly ground black pepper and stir well to combine.

4 Blanch the asparagus in boiling water for 2 minutes or until just cooked. Drain, then refresh in a bowl of cold water. Drain well and add to the couscous, along with the tomato. Gently toss to combine, then transfer to a large bowl or platter.

5 Slice the lamb racks into individual cutlets and arrange on top of the couscous. Scatter the chopped nuts over the top and serve.

1 SERVE =
1 UNIT PROTEIN
1 UNIT DAIRY
1½ UNITS VEGETABLES
½ UNIT FATS

Middle Eastern chickpea and feta salad

SERVES 4 PREP TIME **20 minutes, plus standing time**
COOKING TIME **10 minutes**

Make this delicious salad in advance to allow the flavours to develop.

1 teaspoon ground coriander
1 teaspoon ground sumac
1 teaspoon ground cumin
2 teaspoons olive oil
1 small red onion, finely chopped
2 cloves garlic, crushed
600 g tinned chickpeas, rinsed and drained
80 g reduced-fat feta, roughly chopped
1 small green chilli, thinly sliced
1 small green capsicum (pepper), trimmed, seeded and thinly sliced
3 firm, ripe tomatoes, chopped
1 Lebanese (small) cucumber, diced
small handful mint leaves
small handful coriander leaves
2 tablespoons lemon juice

1 Heat a small frying pan over medium heat. Add the ground spices and roast for 1–2 minutes, shaking the pan regularly until the fragrance fills the air. Transfer to a bowl and set aside.
2 Heat the oil in the frying pan over medium heat and cook the onion for 5 minutes, without browning. Add the garlic and cook for 2 minutes. Add to the spices, season with freshly ground black pepper and mix well. Add the chickpeas and toss to coat in the spice mixture. Set aside for 10 minutes.
3 Meanwhile, combine the remaining ingredients in a large bowl. Add the spiced chickpea mixture, toss to mix, then serve.

1 SERVE =
½ UNIT PROTEIN
1 UNIT BREAD
2 UNITS VEGETABLES
½ UNIT FATS

Pesto and tuna rice salad

SERVES 4 PREP TIME **25 minutes**
COOKING TIME **5 minutes**

This dish works best if it's made with cold cooked rice. However, if you don't have any, just cook the rice, then rinse it under cold water until cool. Serve this salad as a lunch.

2 corn cobs (equivalent to approximately 280 g corn kernels)
180 g cooked basmati rice (or 80 g uncooked rice)
2 teaspoons pesto
1 tablespoon lemon juice
1 tablespoon drained capers, rinsed and roughly chopped
½ red onion, thinly sliced
2 Lebanese (small) cucumbers, diced
2 tablespoons chopped chervil or flat-leaf parsley
200 g tinned tuna in spring water, drained
80 g mixed salad leaves

1 Steam the corn cobs for 5 minutes, or until cooked. Leave to cool slightly, then carefully remove the kernels by slicing down the length of each cob with a sharp knife.
2 Place the rice in a large bowl. Combine the pesto and lemon juice and pour over the rice. Mix well to combine, then add the remaining ingredients and mix gently again. Serve immediately or cover and chill until needed.

1 SERVE =
2 UNITS PROTEIN
1 UNIT BREAD
1½ UNITS VEGETABLES
½ UNIT FATS

Char siu-style pork salad

SERVES 4 PREP TIME **20 minutes, plus marinating time**
COOKING TIME **25 minutes**

80 g thin rice stick noodles
small handful coriander leaves
2 tablespoons lemon juice
2 carrots, cut into long julienne
100 g snowpeas (mange-tout), thinly sliced lengthways
1 red capsicum (pepper), trimmed, seeded and cut into long julienne
3 spring onions, white part only, thinly sliced on the diagonal

CHAR SIU-STYLE PORK

3 tablespoons salt-reduced soy sauce
1½ tablespoons red wine vinegar
1½ tablespoons mirin
1 tablespoon hoisin sauce
2 teaspoons honey
1 teaspoon sesame oil
2 teaspoons finely grated ginger
800 g lean pork fillet, trimmed of fat

This sweet, aromatic salad makes for a delicious dinner.

1 To make the char siu-style pork, combine all the ingredients, except the pork. Place the pork in a shallow dish, pour the marinade over and turn to coat. Marinate in the fridge for at least 3 hours, turning the pork two or three times to ensure it is well flavoured.

2 Preheat the oven to 200°C and place a roasting tin filled with about 4 cm water under the oven shelf you plan to use. Remove the pork from the marinade (reserving the marinade) and pat dry with paper towel. Place the pork on an ovenproof wire rack, then place the rack directly on the oven shelf above the tin of water and roast for 15 minutes. Brush with the reserved marinade, then roast for a further 10 minutes or until just cooked through. Remove and cut into 1 cm thick slices.

3 Meanwhile, cook the rice stick noodles in boiling water for 5 minutes. Drain, then refresh under cold water. Place in a large bowl and combine with the remaining salad ingredients.

4 Place the reserved marinade in a small saucepan over medium heat and simmer for 1 minute. Remove from the heat.

5 Arrange the sliced pork on top of the salad, spoon over some of the reserved marinade and serve.

1 SERVE =
2 UNITS PROTEIN
1 UNIT DAIRY
2½ UNITS VEGETABLES
1½ UNITS FATS

Spiced lamb and feta salad

SERVES 4 PREP TIME **30 minutes, plus marinating time**
COOKING TIME **1 hour 30 minutes**

1 tablespoon olive oil
1 tablespoon lemon juice
1 clove garlic, crushed
½ teaspoon chilli powder
1 teaspoon ground cumin
800 g lean lamb fillet, trimmed of fat
450–500 g beetroot
2 bunches asparagus, trimmed and cut into 3 cm lengths
80 g baby spinach leaves
handful mint leaves, larger leaves torn
80 g feta, crumbled
1 tablespoon white wine vinegar

This is a delicious salad to serve on a warm summer's evening. Lamb and feta go very well together, and here we recommend using regular full-fat feta for its wonderful crumbly texture and intense flavour.

1 Combine 2 teaspoons of the oil with the lemon juice, garlic, chilli, cumin and 1 teaspoon freshly ground black pepper in a small bowl. Rub all over the lamb, then cover and leave to marinate in the fridge for at least 30 minutes, preferably several hours.

2 Meanwhile, preheat the oven to 180°C.

3 Trim the tops and bottoms of the beetroot, then scrub but do not peel. Wrap in foil and bake for 1–1¼ hours or until a skewer goes easily into the beetroot. Cool for 10 minutes, then rub off the skins (wearing rubber gloves, to prevent purple-stained hands). Cut into bite-sized chunks.

4 Steam the asparagus for 3–4 minutes or until tender. Refresh under cold water, then set aside.

5 Preheat a chargrill pan over medium heat. Pat the lamb gently with paper towel to remove any excess marinade. Grill for 5 minutes, then turn over and grill for a further 4 minutes for medium-rare, or until cooked to your liking. Transfer the lamb to a warm plate, cover with foil and set aside for 10 minutes to rest (the lamb will continue to cook during this time).

6 Place the spinach and mint leaves in a bowl, add the beetroot, asparagus and feta and mix gently. Combine the remaining oil with the vinegar and pour over the salad. Toss to combine.

7 Using a sharp knife, slice the lamb on the diagonal and arrange on top of the salad. Serve.

Weeknight dinners

1 SERVE =
2 UNITS PROTEIN
1 UNIT BREAD
1½ UNITS VEGETABLES
1 UNIT FATS

Pasta with seafood, chilli and parsley

SERVES 4 PREP TIME **20 minutes** COOKING TIME **30 minutes**

1 tablespoon olive oil
1 onion, finely chopped
2 sticks celery, finely chopped
2 cloves garlic, crushed
1 small red chilli, seeded and thinly sliced
½ cup (125 ml) white wine
1 × 400 g tin chopped tomatoes
120 g wholegrain pasta
500 g salmon fillet, skin removed and pin-boned, cut into bite-sized pieces
300 g raw peeled prawns
2 tablespoons finely chopped flat-leaf parsley
lemon wedges, to serve

This recipe uses prawns and salmon; to speed things up you could replace this with 800 g marinara mix. Buy 300 g ready-peeled prawns from the supermarket to save time.

1 Heat the oil in a large saucepan over medium heat and cook the onion and celery for 8 minutes until soft. Add the garlic and chilli and cook for a further 2 minutes. Stir in the wine and bring to the boil. Add the tomatoes and return to the boil, then reduce the heat to low–medium and simmer, covered, for 10 minutes.

2 Meanwhile, cook the pasta according to the packet instructions, then drain.

3 Add the salmon to the tomato sauce and cook for 3 minutes. Stir in the prawns, tucking them down into the sauce, and cook for a further 2 minutes or until the prawns are pink and just cooked through. Stir in the parsley, then toss through the pasta and serve with lemon wedges.

1 SERVE =
2 UNITS PROTEIN
1 UNIT BREAD
½ UNIT DAIRY
2 UNITS VEGETABLES
1 UNIT FATS

Wholemeal pasta with tuna sauce

SERVES 4 PREP TIME **20 minutes**
COOKING TIME **15 minutes**

This simple sauce is delicious with a bit of chilli added for an extra kick; however, it's still great without it, so make it to suit your taste. The pasta needs to be added to the sauce while still hot so that it warms the sauce.

800 g tinned tuna in spring water, drained
2 tablespoons lemon juice
2 teaspoons drained capers, rinsed
400 g reduced-fat Greek-style yoghurt
40 g mayonnaise
1 small red chilli, seeded and finely chopped (optional)
120 g wholegrain penne or other short pasta
200 g green beans, trimmed and cut into 5 cm lengths
2 bunches broccolini, stalks and tops cut into 5 cm lengths

1 Place the tuna, lemon juice, capers, yoghurt, mayonnaise and chilli (if using) in a food processor, season well with freshly ground black pepper and blend to a smooth sauce. Transfer to a large bowl.

2 Cook the pasta according to the packet instructions, then drain.

3 Meanwhile, blanch the beans and broccolini stalks together for 4 minutes. Transfer to a bowl with a slotted spoon, then blanch the broccolini tops for 3 minutes. Drain.

4 Drain the pasta, then immediately add to the sauce and toss well to combine. Add the blanched vegetables and serve.

1 SERVE =
2 UNITS PROTEIN (IF SERVED WITH 200 G CHICKEN, BEEF OR FISH)
1 UNIT BREAD
2 UNITS VEGETABLES
1 UNIT FATS

Spaghetti with summer vegetables and herbs ›

SERVES 4 PREP TIME **20 minutes**
COOKING TIME **15 minutes**

Bursting with flavour, this is a light, summery dish with a fresh dash of lemon. Serve with 200 g grilled lean chicken, beef or fish per person for 2 units protein.

90 g wholegrain spaghetti or short pasta
100 g peas (thawed if frozen)
200 g green beans, trimmed and cut into 3 cm lengths
3 bunches asparagus, trimmed and cut into 3 cm lengths
1 tablespoon olive oil
1 tablespoon lemon juice
3 tablespoons mint leaves
2 tablespoons snipped chives
1 tablespoon finely grated parmesan (optional)
lemon wedges, to serve

1 Cook the pasta according to the packet instructions, then drain.

2 Meanwhile, blanch or steam the vegetables separately until tender. Transfer to a large bowl, add the oil, lemon juice, mint and chives and season well with freshly ground black pepper. Toss well to combine, then toss through the pasta.

3 Serve with a scattering of parmesan (if using) and lemon wedges for squeezing over.

1 SERVE =
2 UNITS PROTEIN
1 UNIT BREAD
2 UNITS VEGETABLES
1 UNIT FATS

Pasta with roasted tomatoes, chicken and broccoli

SERVES 4 PREP TIME **15 minutes** COOKING TIME **30 minutes**

1 tablespoon olive oil
2 × 250 g punnets cherry tomatoes
2 zucchinis (courgettes), cut into 1 cm slices
4 cloves garlic, unpeeled
800 g skinless chicken breast fillets, cut into large pieces
120 g wholegrain pasta
250 g broccoli, cut into small florets, stalks sliced
½–1 small red chilli, seeded and finely chopped (optional)
handful basil leaves

Roasting tomatoes brings out their sweetness and makes for a rich sauce, perfect to toss through pasta.

1 Preheat the oven to 180°C.

2 Pour the oil into a large baking dish and place it in the oven. Once the oil is hot, add the tomatoes, zucchini and garlic. Season with plenty of freshly ground black pepper and toss so the vegetables are well coated in the oil and pepper. Roast for 10 minutes, then add the chicken and roast for a further 20 minutes, turning the chicken over after 10 minutes, or until the tomatoes have softened and are starting to blacken and the chicken is cooked through.

3 Meanwhile, cook the pasta according to the packet instructions, then drain.

4 Blanch the broccoli for 2 minutes, then drain and set aside.

5 Remove the garlic and squeeze out the soft flesh into the dish, discarding the skins. Add the broccoli and chilli (if using) and shake to combine. Add the pasta, scatter over the basil leaves and toss again, then serve.

1 SERVE =
2 UNITS PROTEIN
1 UNIT BREAD
2 UNITS VEGETABLES
2 UNITS FATS

Chicken stir-fry with vegetables and rice noodles

SERVES 4 PREP TIME **20 minutes** COOKING TIME **15 minutes**

80 g dried rice noodles
3 tablespoons oyster sauce
1 tablespoon salt-reduced soy sauce
1 tablespoon rice wine vinegar
2 tablespoons vegetable oil
2 cloves garlic, crushed
1 teaspoon finely grated ginger (optional)
800 g skinless chicken breast fillet, thinly sliced
150 g snowpeas (mange-tout), trimmed and halved on the diagonal
140 g baby corn, halved on the diagonal
1 red capsicum (pepper), trimmed, seeded and cut into thin strips
200 g shiitake mushrooms, roughly chopped

Stir-fries are always a winner because once everything is chopped, they can be cooked very quickly. Make sure everything is prepared before you start cooking.

1 Cook the rice noodles in boiling water for 6 minutes or according to the packet instructions. Drain and set aside.

2 Combine the oyster sauce, soy sauce and rice wine vinegar and set aside.

3 Heat 2 teaspoons of the oil in a wok or large frying pan over medium heat. Add the garlic and ginger (if using) and stir-fry for 30 seconds. Add half of the chicken and stir-fry for 3–4 minutes or until just cooked through, then remove from the wok and set aside in a bowl. Heat another 2 teaspoons of the oil and stir-fry the remaining chicken, then transfer to the bowl.

4 Heat 2 teaspoons of the oil in the wok, add the snowpeas, baby corn and capsicum and stir-fry for 2 minutes, then add 2 tablespoons water (carefully, as it may spit). Remove and add to the cooked chicken.

5 Heat the remaining oil, add the mushrooms and stir-fry for 2 minutes, adding 1 tablespoon water. Return the chicken and vegetables to the wok, pour in the sauce and stir-fry for 1 minute, tossing everything around to coat well in the sauce.

6 Serve immediately with the noodles.

1 SERVE =
2 UNITS PROTEIN
1 UNIT BREAD
2 UNITS VEGETABLES
1½ UNITS FATS

Grilled tuna and vegetable skewers with sesame spinach and broccoli

SERVES 4 PREP TIME **25 minutes** COOKING TIME **10 minutes**

2 tablespoons salt-reduced soy sauce
2 tablespoons mirin
1 clove garlic, crushed
800 g tuna fillet, cut into 3 cm cubes
4 spring onions, cut into sixteen 4 cm lengths
16 small brown or button mushrooms
180 g cooked basmati rice (from 80 g uncooked)

SESAME SPINACH AND BROCCOLI
2 teaspoons sesame seeds
2 teaspoons vegetable oil
2 teaspoons sesame oil
1 clove garlic, sliced
1 teaspoon finely grated ginger
300 g broccoli, cut into small florets
2 bunches spinach, washed, tough stalks discarded

These can be threaded onto metal or wooden skewers. If using wooden skewers, soak them in water for 20 minutes before using, to prevent them burning.

1 Combine the soy sauce, mirin and garlic in a small bowl. Place the tuna cubes in a shallow dish and pour the marinade over. Toss to coat, then place in the fridge while you prepare the other ingredients.

2 Preheat a barbecue to medium or a chargrill pan over medium heat. Thread the tuna onto eight skewers, adding two pieces of spring onion and two mushrooms to each skewer. Brush with the marinade and grill for 4–5 minutes, turning regularly and brushing with marinade each time.

3 To make the sesame spinach and broccoli, heat a small frying pan over medium heat and toast the sesame seeds for 1–2 minutes or until golden, shaking the pan regularly. Transfer to a small bowl and set aside. Heat the oils in a wok or large frying pan over medium heat. Add the garlic, ginger and broccoli and stir-fry for 1 minute. Add 2 tablespoons water (carefully, as it may spit) and stir-fry for a further 2 minutes. Add the spinach and stir-fry until almost wilted. Scatter over the sesame seeds.

4 Serve the skewers with the sesame spinach and broccoli and basmati rice.

1 SERVE =
2 UNITS PROTEIN
1 UNIT BREAD
1 UNIT DAIRY
2 UNITS VEGETABLES
2 UNITS FATS

Beef and vegetable pasticcio

SERVES 4 PREP TIME **45 minutes** COOKING TIME **1 hour 30 minutes**

1 tablespoon olive oil
800 g lean minced beef
1 onion, finely chopped
2 sticks celery, finely chopped
2 cloves garlic, crushed
2 carrots, grated
2 zucchinis (courgettes), grated
1 teaspoon dried oregano or mixed dried herbs
400 ml passata
90 g wholegrain short pasta
1 tablespoon reduced-fat olive oil spread
2 tablespoons plain flour
2 cups (500 ml) reduced-fat milk
80 g reduced-fat cheddar, grated

This is real comfort food for all the family and it's good for you as well. Packed full of healthy vegetables, the meat sauce can be prepared the day before and then reheated before combining it with the cheese sauce and pasta. No extra vegies are needed, although some peas would be a lovely addition.

1. Heat 2 teaspoons of the oil in a large heavy-based saucepan over medium heat and cook the mince in two batches, stirring until browned and breaking up any lumps with the back of the spoon. Remove and set aside.
2. Heat the remaining oil in the pan, add the onion and celery and cook for 5 minutes. Stir in the garlic, carrot, zucchini and dried herbs and cook for a further 10 minutes. Return the mince to the pan and add the passata, stirring well. Bring to the boil, then reduce the heat and simmer, covered, for 40 minutes.
3. Meanwhile, cook the pasta according to the packet instructions, then drain.
4. Preheat the oven to 180°C.
5. Melt the reduced-fat spread in a small saucepan over low–medium heat. Stir in the flour and mix until well combined. Cook, without browning, for 1 minute, stirring regularly. Gradually add the milk, whisking well after each addition to prevent lumps forming. Once all the milk has been incorporated and the sauce is smooth, add the cheddar. Stir until the cheddar has melted, then cook for 2 minutes.
6. Place the cooked pasta in the base of a 2 litre capacity baking dish or ovenproof frying pan. Add the meat sauce and stir to combine. Add half the cheese sauce and stir to combine, then pour the remaining sauce over the top and smooth. Place on a baking tray and bake for 30 minutes or until bubbling.
7. Serve with a grinding of freshly ground black pepper.

TIPS

Passata is pureed, sieved tomatoes, available from supermarkets in the pasta sauce section.

This dish can be assembled up to 24 hours in advance and refrigerated, but it will need to cook for an extra 10–15 minutes to ensure it is piping hot.

1 SERVE =
2 UNITS PROTEIN
1 UNIT BREAD
2 UNITS VEGETABLES
1 UNIT FATS

Polenta-coated chicken with gremolata vegetables

SERVES 4 PREP TIME **30 minutes** COOKING TIME **20 minutes**

4 tablespoons sesame seeds
80 g polenta
750 g skinless chicken breast fillet
2 eggs, lightly beaten
cooking oil spray

GREMOLATA VEGETABLES
2 cloves garlic, finely chopped
finely grated zest of 1 lemon
4 tablespoons finely chopped flat-leaf parsley
300 g green beans, trimmed and halved
2 zucchinis (courgettes), sliced and cut into 1 cm pieces

Polenta is a grain made from corn. It's great for coating chicken and, together with the sesame seeds, gives this dish a real crunch.

1 Preheat the oven to 180°C. Line a baking tray with baking paper.

2 Heat a small frying pan over medium heat and toast the sesame seeds for 1–2 minutes or until golden, shaking the pan regularly. Transfer to a small bowl with the polenta and set aside.

3 Slice each chicken breast in half widthways through the centre to form thin slices so they will cook more quickly.

4 Place the beaten egg in a shallow dish. Spread half of the polenta mixture on a plate. Dip a piece of chicken in the egg, then coat lightly in the polenta and place on the baking tray. Continue coating the chicken pieces in this way, using the second batch of polenta when the first runs out (dividing it into two batches prevents it becoming too soggy with egg).

5 Spray the chicken with cooking oil and bake for 15–20 minutes or until cooked through; very thin pieces of chicken will cook in about 15 minutes, thicker ones will take longer.

6 Meanwhile, to make the gremolata vegetables, combine the garlic, lemon zest and parsley in a small bowl. Steam the green beans and zucchini until tender, then place in a bowl and toss through the gremolata to coat.

7 Serve the chicken with the gremolata vegetables.

1 SERVE =
2 UNITS PROTEIN
1 UNIT BREAD
2 UNITS VEGETABLES
2 UNITS FATS

Chilli pork with beans

SERVES 4 PREP TIME **15 minutes** COOKING TIME **1 hour 25 minutes**

1 tablespoon olive oil
800 g lean minced pork
1 large onion, chopped
2 sticks celery, finely chopped
2 cloves garlic, crushed
1 teaspoon chilli powder
1 teaspoon ground cumin
1 teaspoon ground coriander
200 g mushrooms, chopped
1 × 400 g tin cannellini beans, rinsed and drained
2 × 400 g tins chopped tomatoes

This dish can be prepared the day before, then refrigerated overnight and reheated for dinner – this allows for the flavours to develop even further. If you like, serve this with steamed vegetables from your daily allowance.

1. Heat 2 teaspoons of the oil in a large heavy-based saucepan over medium–high heat. Add the mince in two batches and cook until browned, stirring regularly and breaking up any lumps with the back of a wooden spoon. Remove and set aside.
2. Add the remaining oil to the pan and reduce the heat to medium. Add the onion and celery and cook for 8 minutes. Stir in the garlic, chilli powder, cumin and coriander and cook for 1 minute. Add the mushrooms and cook for 2 minutes.
3. Return the mince to the pan with the beans and tomatoes and season well with freshly ground black pepper. Bring to the boil, then reduce the heat to low and simmer, covered, for 30 minutes. After this time, move the lid so it is half-covering the pan, allowing some of the liquid to evaporate. Cook for a further 30 minutes. If at this point the sauce is still runny, remove the lid and cook for a further 10 minutes to reduce it further.
4. Spoon into shallow bowls and serve.

1 SERVE =
2 UNITS PROTEIN
1 UNIT BREAD
3 UNITS VEGETABLES
2 UNITS FATS

Spicy fish and eggplant with potato salad

SERVES 4 PREP TIME **25 minutes** COOKING TIME **20 minutes**

1 tablespoon olive oil
1 tablespoon balsamic vinegar
1 teaspoon ground cumin
¼–½ teaspoon chilli powder
2 cloves garlic, crushed
2 tablespoons chopped herbs, such as coriander, flat-leaf parsley *or* basil
8 small thin eggplants (aubergines) (about 350 g), stalks removed, halved lengthways
4 × 200 g fish fillets, such as snapper, salmon *or* ling, skin removed and pin-boned

POTATO SALAD
400 g waxy potatoes, halved or quartered if large
2 tablespoons lemon juice
1 tablespoon olive oil
1 teaspoon wholegrain mustard
1 baby cos lettuce *or* 200 g mixed salad leaves, torn
3 firm, ripe tomatoes, roughly chopped
1 Lebanese (small) cucumber, cut into chunks

In this recipe the same spice paste is used to flavour the fish and the eggplant. Adjust the amount of chilli to suit your taste.

1 Preheat the oven to 180°C and line two baking trays with baking paper.

2 To make the potato salad, boil or steam the potato until tender. Drain. Combine the lemon juice, oil and mustard and season with freshly ground black pepper. Cut the potatoes into small chunks, then pour the dressing over while still warm and toss to combine. Leave to cool for 10 minutes. Mix together the lettuce leaves, tomato and cucumber, then add to the potato and toss to combine.

3 Meanwhile, combine the oil, vinegar, cumin, chilli powder, garlic, herbs and 1 teaspoon freshly ground black pepper in a small bowl. Cut a criss-cross pattern into the flesh of the eggplant, then brush with half the spice paste. Brush the remaining paste over the fish fillets. Place the fish and eggplant on the prepared trays. Bake the eggplant for 15–20 minutes or until soft. At the same time, bake the fish for 10–15 minutes or until cooked through. Thinner white fillets will cook more quickly than thicker salmon fillets.

4 Serve the fish and eggplant with the potato salad.

1 SERVE =
2 UNITS PROTEIN
1 UNIT BREAD
2 UNITS VEGETABLES
2 UNITS FATS

Stuffed pork schnitzels with tomato sauce

SERVES 4 PREP TIME **25 minutes** COOKING TIME **15 minutes**

40 g semi-dried or sun-dried tomatoes, drained
80 g reduced-fat cream cheese
2 tablespoons snipped chives, plus extra to serve
2 tablespoons chopped flat-leaf parsley
800 g lean pork schnitzels
2 teaspoons olive or vegetable oil
1 × 400 g tin cherry tomatoes
1 clove garlic, crushed
180 g cooked basmati rice (from 80 g uncooked)
300 g steamed green beans

These make a nice change from the traditional pork chop. Thin schnitzels are rolled up around a herby cream-cheese filling and cooked in a rich tomato sauce.

1 Pat the sun-dried tomatoes between sheets of paper towel to remove any excess oil, then finely chop. Beat the cream cheese to soften, then combine with the herbs and sun-dried tomato and season well with freshly ground black pepper.

2 Lay each pork schnitzel on a board. Spread the cream cheese mixture evenly over the schnitzels and roll up (but not too tightly). Secure with a toothpick.

3 Heat the oil in a large frying pan over medium–high heat and fry the schnitzel rolls all over for 2–3 minutes until golden (don't worry if some of the filling comes out - it will just become part of the sauce). Add the tomatoes and garlic to the pan, season with freshly ground black pepper and bring to a simmer. Turn the pork to coat in the sauce, then reduce the heat to medium and cook for a further 8 minutes, turning occasionally. Remove from the heat, cover and leave to stand for 2 minutes, to ensure the pork is cooked all the way through.

4 Serve the pork with the sauce spooned over, accompanied by basmati rice and steamed green beans.

1 SERVE =
2 UNITS PROTEIN
1 UNIT BREAD
½ UNIT VEGETABLES
1½ UNITS FATS

Fish and vegetable parcels with tarragon sauce

SERVES 4 PREP TIME **20 minutes** COOKING TIME **15 minutes**

2 lemons
32 snowpeas (mange-tout)
8 sprigs thyme
4 × 200 g fish fillets, such as snapper, ling or salmon, skin removed and pin-boned
180 g cooked basmati rice (from 80 g uncooked)

TARRAGON SAUCE
2 teaspoons olive oil
2 teaspoons white wine vinegar
1 clove garlic, crushed
1½ tablespoons chopped tarragon
3 tablespoons reduced-fat pouring cream
1 egg yolk

Steaming fish in parcels seals in all the flavours and juices. This sauce is intensely flavoured, so a little goes a long way. Don't make it in advance as it is difficult to reheat. Use your favourite fish fillets for this dish, but remember that fish such as salmon have a stronger flavour than most white fish.

1 Preheat the oven to 180°C.

2 Cut four pieces of foil or baking paper large enough to enclose each fish fillet completely in a parcel. Slice one of the lemons and arrange two slices in the middle of each piece of foil or paper. Top with four snowpeas, a sprinkling of thyme and then a piece of fish. Top with four more snowpeas, the remaining thyme and a slice of lemon. Season well with freshly ground black pepper.

3 Cut the remaining lemon into six wedges and squeeze the juice from two wedges over the fish. Wrap up the fish to enclose, ensuring there are no holes. Place on a baking tray and bake for 10–15 minutes. The actual cooking time will depend on the thickness of the fish – thinner white fish fillets will cook more quickly than salmon. To test, carefully open one parcel and stick a sharp knife into the middle of the fish to see if it is cooked through; if not, return the fish to the oven for a further 5 minutes.

4 Meanwhile, to make the tarragon sauce, combine the oil, vinegar, garlic, tarragon and cream in a small saucepan over low heat. Cook, stirring constantly, for 2 minutes. Stir in the egg yolk and cook for 1 minute, stirring until the sauce thickens slightly.

5 The fish can be served either in or out of the parcels. Spoon a little sauce over each fish and serve with rice. Slice the remaining lemon wedges and serve alongside.

1 SERVE =
2 UNITS PROTEIN
½ UNIT BREAD
2 UNITS VEGETABLES
1 UNIT FATS

Crumbed fish fingers with tomato and watercress salad

SERVES 4 PREP TIME **20 minutes** COOKING TIME **15 minutes**

2 eggs
1 cup (70 g) panko breadcrumbs
750 g white fish fillets, such as flathead or ling, skin removed and pin-boned
cooking oil spray
lemon wedges, to serve

TOMATO AND WATERCRESS SALAD
3 firm, ripe tomatoes, roughly chopped
1 bunch watercress, tough stalks discarded
½ red onion, halved and sliced
1 Lebanese (small) cucumber, halved lengthways and sliced
1 tablespoon olive oil
1 tablespoon balsamic vinegar
1 teaspoon Dijon mustard

Panko are Japanese breadcrumbs and are generally available in the Asian section of larger supermarkets. Serve the fish immediately once cooked, as it will become soggy if left too long.

1 Preheat the oven to 180°C. Line a baking tray with baking paper.

2 Place the eggs in a bowl and beat lightly. Place half the panko breadcrumbs on a shallow plate and season with freshly ground black pepper.

3 Roughly cut the fish into strips or finger-length pieces. Dip each piece of fish into the egg, allowing any excess to drip off, and then coat in the breadcrumbs. Use the second batch of panko when the first runs out – dividing it into two batches prevents it becoming too soggy with egg.

4 Place the crumbed fish on the prepared tray and spray with cooking oil. Bake for 5 minutes, then carefully turn over and bake for a further 5–8 minutes or until the fish is cooked through. The cooking time will depend on the thickness of the fish.

5 Meanwhile, to make the salad, combine the tomato, watercress, onion and cucumber in a bowl. Whisk together the oil, vinegar and mustard and season with freshly ground black pepper. Pour over the salad and toss.

6 Serve the fish and salad with lemon wedges.

TIP Skinless chicken breast fillets can be crumbed in the same way. Cut into thin strips, or halve the chicken breast widthways, then crumb as above. Bake for 10–15 minutes or until cooked through, depending on the thickness of the chicken.

1 SERVE =
1 UNIT PROTEIN
1 UNIT VEGETABLES
1 UNIT FATS

Vegetarian cassoulet

SERVES 4 PREP TIME **15 minutes**
COOKING TIME **45 minutes**

This is a healthier version of the traditional cassoulet. Beans, vegetables and plenty of fresh herbs make it a delicious, hearty dinner.

1 tablespoon olive oil
1 large onion, chopped
2 sticks celery, diced
3 carrots, diced
3 cloves garlic, finely chopped
1 teaspoon paprika
1 sprig rosemary
8 sage leaves
3 × 400 g tins borlotti or cannellini beans, rinsed and drained
1 tablespoon tomato paste (puree)
3 cups (750 ml) boiling water
3 tablespoons chopped flat-leaf parsley

1 Heat the oil in a large saucepan over medium heat. Add the onion, celery and carrot and cook for 5 minutes. Add the garlic, paprika, rosemary and sage and cook for 1 minute.

2 Add the beans, tomato paste and boiling water and stir to combine. Reduce the heat and simmer, covered, for 35 minutes. At this stage the carrot will still have some bite – cook for longer if you prefer softer carrots. Stir in the parsley, then remove from the heat and leave to stand for 5 minutes before serving.

TIP For a healthy, non-vegetarian option, add 200 g (for lunch) or 800 g (for dinner) strips of lean chicken breast fillet when the water is added.

1 SERVE =
2 UNITS PROTEIN
1 UNIT BREAD
2½ UNITS VEGETABLES
1 UNIT FATS

Vegetable fried rice

SERVES 4 PREP TIME **20 minutes**
COOKING TIME **10 minutes**

This fried rice is packed full of vegetables. It's best to use cold, cooked rice for this, so make extra the night before. Alternatively, just cook the rice first and rinse it under cold water, then drain well.

4 eggs, lightly beaten
1 tablespoon salt-reduced soy sauce
2 tablespoons fish sauce
1 tablespoon vegetable oil
2 cloves garlic, sliced
2 teaspoons finely grated ginger
2 zucchinis (courgettes), diced
1 red capsicum (pepper), trimmed, seeded and cut into strips
200 g button mushrooms, roughly chopped
180 g cooked basmati rice (from 80 g uncooked)
750 g firm tofu, cut into 3 cm cubes
100 g bean sprouts, trimmed
3 spring onions, thinly sliced on the diagonal
3 tablespoons chopped coriander

1 Whisk together the eggs, soy sauce and fish sauce and season well with freshly ground black pepper. Set aside.

2 Heat 2 teaspoons of the oil in a wok or large frying pan over medium heat. Add the garlic and ginger and stir-fry for 1 minute. Add the zucchini and capsicum and stir-fry for 2 minutes, then add 2 tablespoons water (carefully, as it may spit). Add the mushroom and stir-fry for 1–2 minutes or until soft. Remove the vegetables from the wok.

3 Heat the remaining oil in the wok. Add the egg mixture and cook for 1 minute, scrambling slightly. Add the cooked rice and tofu and mix well. Cook for 1 minute, then return the vegetables to the wok and toss to combine. Scatter over the bean sprouts, spring onions and coriander and serve.

1 SERVE =
1 UNIT BREAD
2½ UNITS VEGETABLES
2½ UNITS FATS

Barley and mushroom risotto

SERVES 4 PREP TIME **15 minutes**
COOKING TIME **1 hour 15 minutes**

2 tablespoons olive oil
1 onion, chopped
1 leek, trimmed, white part only, washed and thinly sliced
2 carrots, diced
2 cups (500 ml) salt-reduced vegetable or chicken stock
2 cloves garlic, crushed
80 g pearl barley
1 sprig thyme
200 g mixed mushrooms, such as Swiss brown, button and flat, sliced
40 g reduced-fat cream cheese
2 tablespoons chopped flat-leaf parsley

Barley has more of a bite to it than risotto rice so it can be left to simmer for a while without stirring. Although the cooking time looks lengthy, this risotto doesn't require much attention. Serve with 200 g grilled lean chicken or fish or marinated tofu per person for dinner for 2 protein units.

1. Heat 1 tablespoon of the oil in a deep-sided frying pan or saucepan over medium heat. Add the onion, leek and carrot and cook over low heat for 10 minutes, stirring occasionally.
2. Meanwhile, pour the stock into a small saucepan, cover and bring to a simmer.
3. Add the garlic to the vegetables and cook for 1 minute, then add the barley and stir to coat well in the onion mixture. Add the thyme and half of the stock. Stir well, then simmer, covered, for 10 minutes or until most of the stock has been absorbed. Add the remaining stock, stir again and simmer, covered, for 50 minutes or until the barley is tender. Check the liquid level after 40 minutes – if it looks dry, add 2–3 tablespoons water.
4. When the barley is cooked, heat the remaining oil in a frying pan over medium-high heat. Add the mushrooms and plenty of freshly ground black pepper and cook for 3–4 minutes or until tender.
5. Remove the thyme sprig from the risotto. Stir in the cream cheese, then the mushroom and parsley, and serve.

1 SERVE =
2 UNITS PROTEIN
1 UNIT BREAD
3 UNITS VEGETABLES
2 UNITS FATS

Asian mushroom, tofu and vegetable stir-fry

SERVES 4 PREP TIME **20 minutes** COOKING TIME **15 minutes**

600 g firm tofu, cut into 1 cm cubes
2 teaspoons finely grated ginger
3 tablespoons hoisin sauce
3 tablespoons salt-reduced soy sauce
2 tablespoons vegetable oil
4 eggs, lightly beaten
2 cloves garlic, thinly sliced
6 spring onions, cut into 2 cm lengths
200 g broccoli, broken into small florets, stalks sliced
200 g green beans, trimmed and cut into 3 cm lengths
200 g mixed Asian mushrooms, such as shiitake, oyster and enoki, sliced
180 g cooked basmati rice (from 80 g uncooked)

Including a generous amount of mushrooms in a dish is an excellent way to add lots of minerals without adding many kilojoules. If a choice is available, go for firm rather than soft tofu.

1 Place the tofu in a bowl. Combine the ginger, hoisin sauce, soy sauce and 2 tablespoons water and pour over the tofu. Gently toss to coat, then set aside.

2 Heat 1 teaspoon of the oil in a wok or frying pan over medium heat and swirl it around to coat. Add half the beaten egg and swirl to form a thin omelette. Leave it to set, then carefully remove to a board. Repeat with another teaspoon of oil and the remaining egg. Roll each omelette up and cut into thin strips. Set aside.

3 Heat 1 tablespoon of the oil in the wok or pan over medium heat. Add the garlic and spring onion and cook for 1 minute. Add the broccoli and beans and stir-fry for 3 minutes, carefully adding 3–4 tablespoons water during cooking. Transfer to a large bowl.

4 Heat the remaining oil in the wok or pan, add the mushrooms and stir-fry for 1 minute. Add the tofu and sauce and stir-fry for 2 minutes to coat everything in the sauce, adding 1–2 tablespoons water if needed. Return the vegetables to the wok or pan and toss to coat.

5 Serve immediately with rice, topped with the omelette strips.

1 SERVE =
2 UNITS PROTEIN
1 UNIT BREAD
½ UNIT DAIRY
2½ UNITS VEGETABLES
1 UNIT FATS

Greek-style lamb and eggplant bake

SERVES 4 PREP TIME **20 minutes** COOKING TIME **1 hour**

1 tablespoon olive oil
800 g lean minced lamb
1 onion, chopped
2 cloves garlic, crushed
1 eggplant (aubergine), cut into 1 cm cubes
2 zucchinis (courgettes), diced
600 g tinned chopped tomatoes
1 tablespoon chopped oregano *or* 1 teaspoon dried oregano
2 tablespoons chopped flat-leaf parsley, plus extra to serve
1 tablespoon tomato paste (puree)
400 g reduced-fat Greek-style yoghurt
1 egg
180 g cooked basmati rice (from 80 g uncooked)

A fine example of hearty, warming food. Serve it with some steamed green vegetables for a complete meal. You will need a 2 litre capacity baking dish to cook this in – if you don't have one large enough, bake it in two smaller dishes.

1 Heat 2 teaspoons of the oil in a large heavy-based saucepan over medium heat and cook the mince in two batches, stirring until browned and breaking up any lumps with the back of a wooden spoon. Set the cooked mince aside, discarding any liquid in the pan.

2 Heat the remaining oil and cook the onion for 5 minutes. Add the garlic, eggplant, zucchini and 400 g of the tomatoes and simmer for 5 minutes. Return the mince to the pan with the oregano, parsley, tomato paste and remaining tomatoes. Bring to the boil, then move the lid so it is half-covering the pan, allowing some of the liquid to evaporate. Reduce the heat to low and simmer for 20 minutes. If there is still quite a lot of liquid, remove the lid and simmer for a further 5–10 minutes or until reduced.

3 Preheat the oven to 180°C.

4 Beat the yoghurt to loosen, then beat in the egg and season well with freshly ground black pepper.

5 Add the rice to the mince and vegetables and stir to combine. Transfer to a 2 litre capacity baking dish. Spoon the yoghurt sauce evenly over the top and bake for 20 minutes. Leave to stand for 5 minutes, then scatter over some extra parsley.

TIP This dish can be prepared and assembled the day before you wish to eat it. If you do this, increase the baking time by at least 10 minutes to make sure it is piping hot all the way through.

1 SERVE =
2 UNITS PROTEIN
1 UNIT BREAD
2 UNITS VEGETABLES
2 UNITS FATS

Chicken with wilted greens

SERVES 4 PREP TIME **20 minutes** COOKING TIME **50 minutes**

2 tablespoons olive oil
400 g waxy potatoes, cut into wedges
6 sprigs thyme (optional)
1 lemon, cut into eight wedges
800 g skinless chicken breast fillet
1 cup (250 ml) salt-reduced chicken stock
300 g green beans, trimmed
1 clove garlic, crushed
1 small red chilli, seeded and finely chopped (optional)
1 bunch spinach, washed, tough stalks discarded
1 bunch rocket (*or* 60 g wild rocket), roughly torn, plus extra to serve
1 bunch cavolo nero, tough stalks discarded, roughly chopped

Cavolo nero is an Italian black cabbage found in some supermarkets and many fruit and vegetable shops. If it's not available, add an extra bunch of spinach.

1. Preheat the oven to 180°C.
2. Line a small roasting tin with baking paper. Pour in 1½ tablespoons of the oil and place the tin in the oven. Once the oil is hot, add the potato, half the thyme (if using) and three lemon wedges. Season with freshly ground black pepper and toss everything around so the potato is well coated in the oil and pepper. Roast for 45 minutes or until the potato is golden and cooked through, turning once or twice during cooking.
3. Meanwhile, cut each chicken breast in half widthways, then cut the thicker end in half through the centre so that all pieces are of equal thickness.
4. Pour the chicken stock into a roasting tin and add the chicken, four of the lemon wedges and the remaining thyme (if using). Season with freshly ground black pepper and bake for 20–25 minutes, or until the chicken is cooked through.
5. Blanch or steam the green beans until tender. Plunge into cold water to refresh and set aside.
6. When the chicken and potato are cooked, heat the remaining oil in a wok or large frying pan over medium heat. Add the garlic and chilli (if using) and stir-fry for 30 seconds. Add the steamed beans and the leafy greens and stir-fry until the greens are wilted. Transfer to a bowl, squeeze over the juice from the remaining lemon wedge and season with freshly ground black pepper.
7. Scatter some extra rocket over the chicken and potato and serve with the wilted greens.

1 SERVE =
2 UNITS PROTEIN
1½ UNITS BREAD
3 UNITS VEGETABLES
2 UNITS FATS

7/10

Lentil and salmon patties with roasted capsicum salad

SERVES 4 PREP TIME **25 minutes, plus refrigeration time**
COOKING TIME **15 minutes**

- **1 × 420 g tin brown lentils, drained**
- **1 large carrot, grated**
- **2 sticks celery, finely chopped**
- **80 g white cabbage, grated**
- **700 g tinned salmon**
- **2 eggs, lightly beaten**
- **½ cup (35 g) panko breadcrumbs**
- **2 tablespoons olive oil**

ROASTED CAPSICUM SALAD

- **200 g chargrilled red capsicums (peppers), drained well and roughly chopped**
- **1 small red onion, thinly sliced**
- **150 g cherry tomatoes, halved**
- **100 g salad leaves, such as rocket or watercress, large leaves torn**
- **2–4 teaspoons balsamic vinegar**

These patties are delicious warm or cold and any leftovers can be enjoyed for lunch the next day. The recipe calls for roasted chargrilled capsicums from a jar; if they are in oil, pat them dry on a paper towel to remove any excess oil.

1. Combine the lentils, carrot, celery, cabbage and salmon in a large bowl. Add the egg and breadcrumbs and season well with freshly ground black pepper. Form into eight same-sized patties and chill for 10 minutes.
2. To make the salad, combine all the ingredients in a bowl, adding balsamic vinegar to taste.
3. Heat the oil in a large frying pan over low–medium heat, add the lentil patties in two batches and cook for 6–7 minutes on each side or until golden brown.
4. Serve two patties per person with the salad.

TIPS

If you prefer, roast your own capsicums. See recipe on page 180.

You can make your own breadcrumbs – just whiz up some day-old low-GI bread in the food processor.

1 SERVE =
2 UNITS PROTEIN
½ UNIT BREAD
1½ UNITS VEGETABLES
1 UNIT FATS

Grilled chermoula salmon with steamed vegetables

SERVES 4 PREP TIME **20 minutes, plus marinating time**
COOKING TIME **15 minutes**

2 cloves garlic, crushed
2 spring onions, finely chopped
2 tablespoons finely chopped coriander
¼–½ teaspoon dried chilli flakes (optional)
1 teaspoon ground ginger
1 teaspoon ground coriander
1 tablespoon olive oil
3 tablespoons lemon juice
1 × 800 g salmon fillet, skin removed and pin-boned
2 bunches asparagus, trimmed and halved lengthways
2 zucchinis (courgettes), halved and roughly chopped
200 g frozen peas
lime wedges, to serve

Although the marinating time here is only 30 minutes, it adds a delicious flavour to the fish. If you're in a rush, even 10 minutes will make a difference. Don't be tempted to marinate for longer as the lemon juice will start to 'cook' the fish.

1 Combine the garlic, spring onion, coriander, chilli flakes (if using), ground spices, oil and lemon juice in a small bowl. Place the salmon in a shallow dish, spoon the marinade over and turn the fish to coat. Chill in the fridge for 30 minutes (if possible).

2 When you're nearly ready to eat, steam the asparagus and zucchini for 3 minutes or until tender. Blanch the peas, then drain well. Combine all the vegetables in a serving bowl or set aside to serve with the salmon.

3 Meanwhile, preheat the oven grill to high and line the grill tray with foil. Grill the salmon for 10–15 minutes (do not turn) or until cooked through in the thickest part. The exact cooking time will depend on the thickness of the fish. Do not overcook the fish or it will become dry.

4 Serve the salmon with the steamed vegetables and lime wedges for squeezing over.

TIP The salmon can also be marinated in a ziplock bag. Place the fish and all the marinade ingredients in the bag, seal and refrigerate until needed.

Barbecues and picnics

1 SERVE =
1 UNIT BREAD
1 UNIT DAIRY
1 UNIT VEGETABLES
1 UNIT FATS

Spinach and feta filo pastry triangles

SERVES 4 PREP TIME **30 minutes** COOKING TIME **35 minutes**

1 bunch spinach, washed, tough stalks discarded
80 g reduced-fat feta, finely chopped
3 tablespoons pine nuts, toasted
30 g rocket leaves, roughly torn
1 small egg, lightly beaten
1 teaspoon finely grated lemon zest
4 pitted kalamata olives, finely chopped
8 sheets filo pastry
cooking oil spray
tangy tomato chutney or relish, to serve (optional)

These hard-to-resist pastries make the perfect snack to take on a picnic. If using fresh filo pastry, you can make these in advance and freeze the triangles for later use, then thaw before baking.

1 Rinse the spinach leaves well, then place in a large saucepan with only the water clinging to the leaves (no extra water). Cook over high heat for 2–3 minutes, shaking the pan regularly and turning the spinach until it has wilted. Turn out into a sieve and cool for 5 minutes, then squeeze out as much water as possible.

2 Chop the spinach and place in a bowl with the feta, pine nuts, rocket, egg, lemon zest and olives. Season with freshly ground black pepper and mix well.

3 Preheat the oven to 180°C. Line a baking tray with baking paper.

4 Place the sheets of filo pastry in a neat pile on a work surface and cut into three long strips (each about 9.5 cm wide). Take a strip of pastry and spray lightly with cooking oil. Place a second strip on top and spray. (Keep the remaining sheets covered with a damp tea towel to prevent them from drying out.) Dollop a tablespoon of filling onto the pastry a few centimetres from the top. Fold the pastry over the filling diagonally to create a triangle, then continue folding the parcel over itself, keeping the triangle shape. Spray with cooking oil and place on the prepared tray.

5 Repeat with the remaining pastry (using two strips each time) and filling to make twelve triangles. Bake for 30 minutes until golden brown and crisp. Serve with tomato chutney or relish, if you like.

1 SERVE =
2 UNITS PROTEIN
2 UNITS VEGETABLES
2 UNITS FATS

Lemon and herb chicken with fennel salad

SERVES 4 PREP TIME **40 minutes, plus marinating time**
COOKING TIME **10 minutes**

2 tablespoons lemon juice
2 teaspoons olive oil
2 cloves garlic, crushed
1 tablespoon chopped oregano leaves *or* 1 teaspoon dried oregano
1 × 3 cm piece ginger, finely grated
800 g skinless chicken breast fillet
cooking oil spray

FENNEL SALAD
1 bulb fennel, trimmed, feathery fronds reserved
2 Lebanese (small) cucumbers, sliced lengthways using a vegetable peeler
30 g snowpea (mange-tout) sprouts
2 teaspoons olive oil
1 tablespoon sherry or white wine vinegar
80 g pitted black olives, roughly chopped

Start preparing this a few hours before dinner to allow time for both the chicken and the salad to marinate.

1 Combine the lemon juice, oil, garlic, oregano and ginger in a small bowl and season well with freshly ground black pepper. Cut the chicken breasts in half widthways through the centre to form thin slices so they will cook more quickly. Place in a shallow dish and pour over the marinade. Toss to coat several times, then leave to marinate in the fridge for at least 2 hours and up to 12 hours.

2 Meanwhile, to make the salad, slice the fennel bulb in half top to bottom, then place it on a board, cut-side down, and thinly slice. Place in a large bowl, separating the slices as you go. Add the cucumber and snowpea sprouts. Combine the oil and vinegar and season with freshly ground black pepper. Pour over the salad, then toss well. Scatter over the olives, then set aside for at least 30 minutes to allow the flavours to develop.

3 Spray a barbecue grill plate with cooking oil, then preheat to medium. Pat the chicken lightly with paper towel, then grill for 4–5 minutes on each side or until cooked through. The cooking time will depend on the thickness of the chicken. Do not overcook or the chicken will become dry.

4 Thickly slice the chicken and serve with the fennel salad, with the reserved fronds scattered over.

TIP For a picnic, the chicken can be cooked in advance. Combine with the salad just before serving.

1 SERVE =
2 UNITS PROTEIN
1 UNIT BREAD
1½ UNITS VEGETABLES
3 UNITS FATS

Spiced butterflied leg of lamb with corn and tomato salad

SERVES 6 PREP TIME **30 minutes, plus marinating and resting time**
COOKING TIME **25 minutes**

1 × 1.7 kg leg of lamb, butterflied (1.2 kg without the bone)
1½ tablespoons olive oil
1 tablespoon finely grated ginger
1 teaspoon ground coriander
1 teaspoon ground cumin
1 teaspoon hot paprika
2 cloves garlic, sliced

CORN AND TOMATO SALAD
3 corn cobs
4 firm, ripe tomatoes, roughly chopped
120 g baby spinach leaves
1 small red onion, halved and thinly sliced
60 g unsalted roasted cashews, roughly chopped
1½ tablespoons olive oil
1 tablespoon wholegrain mustard
1 tablespoon white wine vinegar

This is a dish for when you are feeding a group of friends or family for dinner. To save time, ask your butcher to remove the bone and butterfly the lamb leg for you. If you can, marinate the lamb the day before or at least in the morning, so the spice rub has a chance to really penetrate the meat.

1 Trim any visible fat from the lamb. Combine the oil, ginger, ground spices and 1 teaspoon freshly ground black pepper in a small bowl. Rub all over the lamb. Make several shallow slits in the meat and push a slice of garlic into each one. Set aside, covered, in the fridge to marinate for at least 2 hours and up to 24 hours.

2 Preheat a barbecue to medium. Add the marinated lamb and cook for 15 minutes, then turn over and cook for a further 10 minutes. If the barbecue has a hood, close it while you cook the second side. At this stage, the meat should be fairly well cooked on the outside and pink in the middle (if you prefer your meat well done, continue to cook for a further 5 minutes or until cooked to your liking). Remove from the heat, cover with foil and leave to rest for 10 minutes; the meat will continue to cook during this time.

3 Meanwhile, to make the salad, steam or microwave the corn for 3–5 minutes. Place on the hot barbecue and cook, turning regularly, until lightly blackened. Using a sharp knife, carefully remove the kernels by slicing down the length of each cob, and place on a serving platter or in a bowl with the tomato, spinach, onion and most of the cashews. Whisk together the oil, mustard and vinegar and season well with freshly ground black pepper. Pour over the salad and toss to coat.

4 Cut the lamb into thick slices and arrange over the salad. Scatter over the remaining cashews and serve.

1 SERVE =
½ UNIT PROTEIN
1 UNIT BREAD
1 UNIT DAIRY
¾ UNIT FRUIT
½ UNIT VEGETABLES
1½ UNITS FATS

Barbecued prawn and watermelon salad

SERVES 4 PREP TIME **15 minutes**
COOKING TIME **3 minutes**

200 g raw peeled prawns
80 g reduced-fat feta, diced
450 g watermelon, cut into bite-sized pieces
1 × 400 g tin cannellini beans, rinsed and drained
100 g mixed salad leaves, rocket or watercress
1 tablespoon olive oil
1 tablespoon white wine vinegar
1 teaspoon dried oregano
20 g pistachios, roughly chopped

This is a simple salad, full of clean flavours and perfect for lunch. If you are cooking the prawns beforehand, then add them and the nuts to the remaining ingredients just before you're ready to eat. Buy 200 g ready-peeled prawns from the supermarket to save time.

1 Preheat a barbecue or chargrill pan to medium–hot. Add the prawns and cook for 3 minutes or until pink and just cooked through, turning once. Cut each prawn into three pieces and set aside.

2 Combine the feta, watermelon, cannellini beans and salad leaves on a serving platter. Whisk the oil, vinegar and oregano together, then drizzle over the salad. Top with the prawns and pistachios and serve.

TIP If serving this for dinner, double the quantity of prawns (this provides 1 protein unit per serve).

1 SERVE =
2 UNITS PROTEIN
1½ UNITS VEGETABLES
1 UNIT FATS

Hoisin-marinated pork kebabs with chilli dipping sauce

SERVES 4 PREP TIME **40 minutes, plus marinating time**
COOKING TIME **10 minutes**

3 tablespoons hoisin sauce
2 tablespoons salt-reduced soy sauce
2 tablespoons rice wine vinegar or dry sherry
800 g pork neck fillet, cut into 3 cm cubes
1 small red onion, cut into eight wedges
8 small brown mushrooms
2 zucchinis (courgettes), cut into 1 cm thick slices
1 red capsicum (pepper), trimmed, seeded and cut into 3 cm squares
cooking oil spray

CHILLI DIPPING SAUCE
40 g mayonnaise
½ small red chilli, seeded and finely chopped
1 tablespoon finely chopped coriander
3 teaspoons lemon juice

Each of these kebabs is a feast on a stick! Juicy marinated pork is lined up next to mushrooms, onion, zucchini and capsicum. If you are using wooden skewers, soak them in water for 20 minutes before cooking to prevent them burning on the barbecue.

1 Combine the hoisin sauce, soy sauce, vinegar or sherry and 1 teaspoon freshly ground black pepper in a bowl. Add the pork and toss to coat. Cover and leave to marinate in the fridge for at least 1 hour and up to 24 hours.
2 Meanwhile, to make the dipping sauce, combine all the ingredients in a small bowl. Add 1 teaspoon water and set aside.
3 Thread the pork onto eight skewers, alternating each cube of pork with a piece of vegetable. Spray lightly with cooking oil.
4 Preheat a barbecue to medium and cook the kebabs, turning regularly, for 10 minutes or until the pork is cooked. Serve with the chilli dipping sauce.

1 SERVE =
2 UNITS PROTEIN
1 UNIT VEGETABLES
1 UNIT FATS

Chinese-style barbecued chicken with cucumber salad

SERVES 4 PREP TIME **25 minutes, plus marinating time**
COOKING TIME **20 minutes**

4 cloves garlic, crushed
1 teaspoon Chinese five-spice powder
2 teaspoons sesame oil
1 tablespoon Chinese rice wine or white vinegar
1½ tablespoons salt-reduced soy sauce
2 teaspoons finely grated ginger
800 g skinless chicken breast fillet
cooking oil spray
lime halves, to serve

CUCUMBER SALAD
2 Lebanese (small) cucumbers
1 clove garlic, crushed
2 small green chillies, seeded and finely chopped
2 teaspoons vegetable oil
2 tablespoons white wine vinegar
2 tablespoons salt-reduced soy sauce
2 firm, ripe tomatoes, sliced into very thin wedges, seeds discarded

This dish can either be served at a barbecue or cooked, packaged and taken on a picnic. The cucumber salad adds a crisp, fresh contrast to the intense flavours in the marinade.

1 Combine the garlic, five-spice powder, oil, vinegar, soy sauce, ginger and 1 teaspoon freshly ground black pepper in a small bowl. Place the chicken in a shallow bowl. Pour over the marinade, turn a few times to coat the chicken, then cover and marinate in the fridge for at least 30 minutes and up to 24 hours.

2 Meanwhile, to make the salad, halve the cucumbers and thickly slice on the diagonal. Place in a bowl with the remaining ingredients (except the tomato) and toss to coat. Set aside for 30 minutes.

3 Spray the barbecue grill plate with cooking oil, then preheat to medium. Remove the chicken from the marinade, allowing any excess to drip off, and pat dry with paper towel. Grill the chicken, turning, for 8–10 minutes or until cooked through. The cooking time will depend on the thickness of the chicken. Do not overcook, or the chicken will become dry.

4 Just before serving, add the tomato wedges to the salad and gently toss to combine. Thickly slice the chicken and serve with the salad and lime halves for squeezing over.

1 SERVE =
2 UNITS PROTEIN
½ UNIT DAIRY

Barbecued prawns with minty yoghurt dip

SERVES 4 PREP TIME **30 minutes, plus marinating time**
COOKING TIME **4 minutes**

1 cup (250 ml) reduced-fat coconut-flavoured evaporated milk
1 × 10 cm piece lemongrass, trimmed and finely chopped
2 kaffir lime leaves, thinly sliced
1 tablespoon fish sauce
1 red chilli, seeded and finely chopped (optional)
800 g raw peeled prawns, with tails intact
lemon wedges, to serve

MINTY YOGHURT DIP
200 g reduced-fat Greek-style yoghurt
2 teaspoons finely chopped mint
1 small clove garlic, crushed
1 tablespoon lemon juice

Once the prawns have been marinated, this dish can be cooked and served very quickly. Buy 800 g ready-peeled prawns from the supermarket to save time. The marinade can also be used to flavour lean chicken fillets, pork loin or lean lamb cutlets.

1 Combine the evaporated milk, lemongrass, kaffir lime leaves, fish sauce and chilli (if using) in a bowl. Add the prawns and toss gently to coat, then cover and marinate in the fridge for 30–60 minutes.

2 Meanwhile, to make the yoghurt dip, combine all the ingredients in a small bowl.

3 Preheat a barbecue grill plate to hot. Remove the prawns from the marinade, allowing any excess to drip off, and pat dry with paper towel (this prevents any remaining marinade burning). Cook, turning once, for 3–4 minutes or until the prawns are pink and just cooked through. Serve immediately with the yoghurt dip and lemon wedges alongside.

TIP This dip is also delicious served with crudites, such as carrot, celery and cucumber sticks, radishes and cherry tomatoes.

1 SERVE =
2 UNITS PROTEIN
¼ UNIT BREAD
1½ UNITS VEGETABLES
½ UNIT FATS

Vegetable and herb meatloaf

SERVES 4 PREP TIME **30 minutes** COOKING TIME **1 hour 5 minutes**

2 teaspoons olive oil
1 large onion, finely chopped
2 cloves garlic, crushed
2 sticks celery, finely chopped
1 small red capsicum (pepper), trimmed, seeded and finely diced
1 large zucchini (courgette), finely grated
800 g lean minced beef
200 g tinned chopped tomatoes
½ cup (35 g) breadcrumbs (made from day-old low-GI bread)
2 tablespoons chopped flat-leaf parsley
3 tablespoons chopped basil
1 egg, lightly beaten
green salad, to serve

Packed full of vegetables and served with a crisp green salad, this is ideal picnic food.

1 Preheat the oven to 180°C. Line a 22 cm × 8 cm loaf tin with baking paper.

2 Heat the oil in a large frying pan over medium heat, then add the onion, garlic, celery and capsicum and cook for 5 minutes or until softened. Transfer to a large bowl and add the zucchini, mince, tomatoes, breadcrumbs, parsley, basil and beaten egg. Season well with freshly ground black pepper and mix everything together with your hands.

3 Transfer the meatloaf mixture to the prepared tin and smooth the top. Bake for 1 hour.

4 Once cooked, leave the meatloaf in the tin for 10 minutes to allow some of the juices to be re-absorbed. Carefully turn out onto a plate with a lip (as there may be more juices) and cut into slices. If taking on a picnic, leave it in the tin and slice when you're ready to eat. Serve with a green salad.

TIPS

This also makes an ideal family dinner. Serve with a selection of two or three different-coloured vegetables.

Any leftover slices of meatloaf are delicious the next day served in a wrap or bread roll with salad.

1 SERVE =
½ UNIT BREAD
1 UNIT DAIRY
2 UNITS VEGETABLES
2 UNITS FATS

Mini vegetable tarts

SERVES 4 PREP TIME **40 minutes** COOKING TIME **40 minutes**

2 tablespoons olive oil
3 large cloves garlic
2 red capsicums (peppers), trimmed, seeded and cut into large chunks
2 red onions, each cut into 8 wedges
2 zucchinis (courgettes), cut into 2 cm thick slices
16 small Swiss brown mushrooms
4 sheets filo pastry
cooking oil spray
80 g reduced-fat cream cheese
16 basil leaves, eight finely chopped, eight left whole

These yummy little tarts are delicious to eat and beautiful to look at. Serve them as an accompaniment to grilled fish or chicken for protein. You will need eight holes of a twelve-hole, ½ cup (125 ml) capacity, muffin tray for this recipe.

1 Preheat the oven to 180°C.

2 Put the oil and garlic cloves into a large roasting tin and place in the oven to heat up. Once the oil is hot, add the capsicum, onion and zucchini. Season with freshly ground black pepper and toss so the vegetables are well coated in the oil and pepper. Roast for 20 minutes, then add the mushrooms, shake the tin again and roast for a further 20 minutes or until the vegetables are just starting to blacken around the edges. Remove the garlic and squeeze out the soft flesh, discarding the skins, then set aside.

3 Meanwhile, take a piece of filo and place on a clean work surface, with the longer side along the bottom. Fold it in half left to right, then fold it in half top to bottom, then left to right again, to form smaller squares. Carefully cut along all the seams to form eight squares. Repeat with the other pieces of filo, keeping them covered while you work to stop them drying out. Spray a square of filo with cooking oil then place a second square on top to form a star shape. Repeat with two more pieces of pastry, then gently press into one hole of the muffin tray. Repeat with the remaining pastry squares until you have eight pastry cups. Bake for 10 minutes or until golden brown. Remove and leave to cool.

4 Combine the cream cheese, chopped basil, garlic flesh and some freshly ground black pepper. Divide the mixture among the cooled pastry cases, then top with the roasted vegetables. Garnish each tart with a basil leaf. Serve warm or cold.

TIP If you're making these in advance to take on a picnic, leave the tarts in the muffin tin to make transporting them easier.

1 SERVE =
½ UNIT BREAD
1 UNIT DAIRY
2 UNITS VEGETABLES
2 UNITS FATS

Feta, olive and tomato bread cups with rocket and radicchio salad

SERVES 4 PREP TIME **20 minutes** COOKING TIME **30 minutes**

375 g cherry tomatoes
1 tablespoon olive oil
2 pieces low-GI mountain bread
80 g reduced-fat feta, crumbled
3 tablespoons pitted kalamata olives, sliced

ROCKET AND RADICCHIO SALAD
1 small head radicchio
60 g rocket leaves
1 tablespoon balsamic vinegar
1 tablespoon sherry vinegar
3 teaspoons olive oil

You will need eight holes of a 12-hole, 1 cup (250 ml) capacity muffin tray to make the bread cups. If you prefer, use reduced-fat ricotta instead of the feta.

1. Preheat the oven to 180°C.
2. Place the tomatoes in a roasting tin, drizzle over 2 teaspoons of the oil, season with freshly ground black pepper and shake the tin so the tomatoes are evenly coated. Roast for 30 minutes or until the tomatoes are softened and starting to blacken. Remove from the oven.
3. Meanwhile, cut each piece of mountain bread into four squares. Brush lightly with oil, then place each square into a muffin hole, pressing down firmly but gently into the base and side so the bread keeps its cup shape. Bake at the same temperature as the tomatoes for 5 minutes or until golden. Remove and leave to cool slightly.
4. To make the salad, remove the tough outer leaves of the radicchio, halve lengthways and remove the core. Roughly chop the leaves, then place in a bowl with the rocket. Whisk together the vinegars and oil and season with freshly ground black pepper. Pour over the salad and toss to coat.
5. To serve, divide the feta among the eight bread cups and top with the roasted tomatoes and olives. Serve warm or cold with the salad.

TIP The bread cups can be prepared a day ahead and stored in an airtight container. Fill just before serving.

1 SERVE =
½ UNIT PROTEIN
1½ UNITS VEGETABLES
1 UNIT FATS

Barbecued tuna steaks with snowpea and baby corn salad

SERVES 4 PREP TIME **25 minutes, plus marinating time**
COOKING TIME **15 minutes**

2 teaspoons ground sumac
2 teaspoons olive oil
1 tablespoon lemon juice
200 g tuna steak
lemon wedges, to serve

SNOWPEA AND BABY CORN SALAD
230 g baby corn
200 g snowpeas (mange-tout), trimmed
40 g snowpea (mange-tout) sprouts
1 teaspoon finely grated ginger
2 teaspoons mirin
1 teaspoon sesame oil
1 teaspoon olive oil
2 tablespoons lemon juice

Ground sumac comes from the seeds of the reddish-purple sumac berry and has a subtle lemon flavour. It is used widely in Middle Eastern cooking, and also makes an appearance in North African cooking. To serve this for dinner, increase the amount of tuna to 800 g (2 protein units per serve).

1 Combine the sumac, oil, lemon juice and 1 teaspoon freshly ground black pepper in a bowl. Place the tuna steak in a shallow dish. Brush all over with the marinade, then cover and refrigerate for at least 30 minutes and up to 2 hours.

2 Meanwhile, to make the salad, steam the baby corn for 5 minutes. Transfer to a bowl with the snowpeas and snowpea sprouts. Combine the remaining ingredients in a small bowl. Immediately spoon some over the warm vegetables and toss well to coat in the dressing. Set aside.

3 Preheat a barbecue to medium–hot. Cook the tuna steak for 5–6 minutes each side or until cooked on the outside but still rare in the middle. The cooking time will depend on the thickness of the fish and the heat of the barbecue. Set aside to rest for 5 minutes.

4 Slice the tuna and serve warm or cold with the salad, remaining dressing and lemon wedges alongside.

TIP If you like, you could also add asparagus to the salad. Trim 2 bunches of asparagus and cut the spears into 4 cm lengths, then add to the steamer with the baby corn.

1 SERVE =
2 UNITS PROTEIN
¼ UNIT DAIRY
½ UNIT FRUIT
1 UNIT VEGETABLES

Tikka salmon with mango salsa

SERVES 4 PREP TIME **30 minutes, plus marinating time**
COOKING TIME **8 minutes**

1 small red onion, halved
2 cloves garlic, crushed
1 teaspoon ground coriander
1 teaspoon ground chilli
1 tablespoon garam masala
1 teaspoon ground cardamom
2 tablespoons tomato paste (puree)
200 g reduced-fat Greek-style yoghurt
4 × 200 g salmon fillets, skin removed and pin-boned
lime wedges or halves, to serve

MANGO SALSA
1 small just-ripe mango, diced
1 firm, ripe tomato, diced
½ red chilli, seeded and finely chopped (optional)
2 tablespoons chopped coriander
1 tablespoon lime juice

This mango salsa is bursting with summery flavours, making it the ideal accompaniment to the salmon.

1 Roughly chop one half of the onion and place in a spice grinder with the garlic, spices and tomato paste and pulse until a paste forms. (If you don't have a spice grinder, finely chop the onion half then mix everything together well.) Place in a small bowl, add the yoghurt and stir to combine.

2 Place the salmon pieces in a shallow bowl and spoon over the marinade, rubbing it all over the fish. Cover and leave to marinate in the fridge for at least 1 hour and up to 8 hours.

3 Meanwhile, to make the mango salsa, place all the ingredients in a small bowl. Finely dice the remaining onion half and stir through the salsa.

4 Preheat a barbecue to hot. Remove the salmon from the marinade and scrape off any excess. Cook for 4 minutes, then turn and cook for a further 3–4 minutes or until the salmon is just cooked but still a little pink in the middle.

5 Flake the salmon into large pieces and serve with the mango salsa and lime wedges.

TIPS

The salmon can be cooked in advance and packed up to take on a picnic. Combine with the salsa just before serving.

This marinade also goes beautifully with chicken. Cut 800 g skinless chicken breast fillet into bite-sized pieces, marinade them as above, then barbecue until cooked through.

1 SERVE =
2 UNITS PROTEIN
1 UNIT BREAD
¼ UNIT DAIRY
1½ UNITS VEGETABLES
2 UNITS FATS

Spicy lamb kofta with couscous salad

SERVES 4 PREP TIME **35 minutes, plus standing time**
COOKING TIME **20 minutes**

1 teaspoon ground coriander
1 teaspoon ground cumin
2 teaspoons olive or canola oil, plus extra for brushing
1 small onion, finely chopped
2 cloves garlic, crushed
800 g lean minced lamb
4 tablespoons chopped coriander
4 tablespoons chopped mint
2 teaspoons harissa paste
200 g reduced-fat Greek-style yoghurt, to serve

COUSCOUS SALAD
80 g couscous
1½ tablespoons olive oil
2 firm, ripe tomatoes, diced
2 Lebanese (small) cucumbers, diced
small handful flat-leaf parsley, finely chopped
small handful mint, finely chopped
½ red onion, finely diced
2 tablespoons lemon juice

Harissa is made from chillies, caraway seeds and other spices. This fiery, bright-red paste can be bought from delis and some supermarkets. Once opened, store it in the fridge for up to 2 months.

1 Heat a small frying pan over medium–high heat. Add the ground spices and dry-fry for 1 minute, shaking the pan regularly so they do not burn, then tip into a large bowl.

2 Heat the oil in the pan, then reduce the heat to low–medium and cook the onion and garlic for 5 minutes or until softened but not browned. Add to the spices, along with the mince, chopped herbs and harissa. Mix well with your hands for 3–4 minutes or until the ingredients are thoroughly combined. Form into eight fat sausage shapes, then chill in the fridge until you're ready to cook them.

3 To make the couscous salad, bring 100 ml water to the boil in a small saucepan. Add the couscous and fork through the grains to separate them. Remove the pan from the heat, cover and leave to stand for 2 minutes. Add 2 teaspoons of the oil. Return to a very low heat and cook for 3 minutes, continuing to fork through the grains. Transfer to a bowl, add the remaining oil and the remaining salad ingredients and mix well. Set aside for 30 minutes to allow the flavours to develop.

4 Preheat a barbecue to hot. Brush the kofta with a little extra oil to prevent them sticking, and cook for 10–15 minutes or until nicely browned on the outside and just cooked in the middle.

5 Serve the kofta with the couscous salad and yoghurt alongside.

TIP Replace the lamb with minced beef, if you prefer.

1 SERVE =
2 UNITS PROTEIN
1 UNIT BREAD
1½ UNITS VEGETABLES
1 UNIT FATS

Spicy Sichuan barbecued beef with noodle salad

SERVES 4 PREP TIME **45 minutes, plus marinating and resting time**
COOKING TIME **10 minutes**

1 teaspoon Sichuan pepper
3 cloves garlic
1 stalk lemongrass, white part only, roughly chopped
2 long red chillies, seeded and roughly chopped
2 teaspoons ground coriander
2 teaspoons canola or vegetable oil
800 g beef fillet

NOODLE SALAD
80 g rice vermicelli noodles
handful coriander leaves
handful mint leaves
1 red chilli, seeded and thinly sliced
1 tablespoon lime juice
2 teaspoons vegetable oil
150 g snowpeas (mange-tout), thinly sliced on the diagonal
2 spring onions, cut into 4 cm lengths, thinly shredded

It only takes a couple of minutes to dry-fry the Sichuan pepper, but it makes a big difference to the flavour of the dish.

1 Heat a small frying pan over high heat. Add the pepper and dry-fry for 1–2 minutes, shaking the pan regularly. Transfer to a spice grinder or small blender along with the garlic, lemongrass, chilli and coriander, then grind to a paste. Transfer to a small bowl, stir in the oil and mix to combine.
2 Rub the spice paste all over the beef, then cover and marinate in the fridge for at least 1 hour and up to 12 hours.
3 To make the salad, soak the noodles in boiling water for 5 minutes or until softened. Drain and rinse under cold water, then drain again and place in a large bowl with the remaining ingredients and mix well.
4 Preheat a barbecue to medium-hot. Add the beef and cook for 4–5 minutes each side for medium-rare or until cooked to your liking. The cooking time will depend on the thickness of the beef. Transfer to a plate, cover with foil and leave to rest for 5 minutes.
5 Slice the beef and serve with the noodle salad.

TIP If you don't feel like firing up the barbecue, the beef can also be chargrilled or grilled.

1 SERVE =
2 UNITS PROTEIN
1 UNIT VEGETABLES

Vietnamese pork meatballs with lime dipping sauce

SERVES 4 PREP TIME **35 minutes, plus refrigerating time**
COOKING TIME **10 minutes**

800 g lean minced pork
1 small red chilli, finely chopped
1 × 6 cm piece lemongrass, finely chopped
3 cloves garlic, crushed
1½ tablespoons fish sauce
3 tablespoons finely chopped mint
3 tablespoons finely chopped coriander

LIME DIPPING SAUCE
2 tablespoons fish sauce
½ small red chilli, seeded and finely chopped
1½ tablespoons lime juice
1 teaspoon sugar

TO SERVE
crisp lettuce leaves
100 g bean sprouts
handful mint leaves

This recipe is the epitome of delicious, sunny-weather food: aromatic meatballs wrapped in crunchy lettuce leaves and served with a sweet and spicy dipping sauce. These meatballs can either be cooked beforehand or at a barbecue as they are delicious hot or cold.

1 Place the pork, chilli, lemongrass, garlic, fish sauce and chopped herbs in a bowl and mix with your hands until the ingredients are well combined. Form into sixteen meatballs, then cover and chill for 30 minutes.

2 To make the lime dipping sauce, place all the ingredients in a small bowl and stir to dissolve the sugar.

3 Shortly before you're ready to serve, arrange the lettuce leaves, bean sprouts and mint leaves on a serving plate.

4 Preheat a barbecue to medium–hot. Cook the meatballs for 8–10 minutes, turning regularly, until just cooked through. Be careful not to overcook them, otherwise they will become dry.

5 To serve, place a meatball in a lettuce leaf with some bean sprouts and mint. Spoon over a little of the sauce, then wrap up and eat.

TIP For ease, you can also thread these meatballs onto metal or soaked wooden skewers to cook; thread four onto each skewer.

1 SERVE =
½ UNIT PROTEIN
1 UNIT DAIRY
1 UNIT VEGETABLES
½ UNIT FATS

Caramelised onion frittata with feta and spring vegetables

SERVES 8 PREP TIME **15 minutes** COOKING TIME **25 minutes**

2 teaspoons olive oil
1 large onion, thinly sliced
1 bunch asparagus, trimmed and cut into 2 cm lengths
100 g fresh or frozen peas
8 eggs, lightly beaten
3 tablespoons reduced-fat milk
1 teaspoon dried oregano
80 g reduced-fat feta, roughly chopped

Prepare this beautiful frittata in advance, then either cut it into wedges and wrap, or leave in the frying pan to make it easy to transport. This meal provides ½ protein unit per serve, so enjoy it for lunch. If you like, serve with mixed salad leaves from your daily allowance.

1 Heat the oil in a 20 cm non-stick frying pan over low–medium heat. Add the onion and cook gently for 10–15 minutes or until golden and caramelised, stirring occasionally.

2 Meanwhile, blanch or steam the asparagus and peas until tender.

3 Whisk together the egg, milk and oregano and season well with freshly ground black pepper.

4 Preheat the oven grill to high.

5 Once the onions are caramelised, increase the heat slightly and pour in the egg mixture, moving the pan so the base is covered with egg. Cook for 1 minute then, using a fork or spatula, gradually draw in the egg from the side, allowing the uncooked egg to flow to the side. Scatter over the vegetables and feta and cook for a further 2 minutes.

6 Place the pan under the hot grill for 3–4 minutes until the top is puffed and golden (wrapping the pan handle in foil if necessary). Leave the frittata to cool in the pan, then turn it out and cut it into pieces to serve.

1 SERVE =
½ UNIT PROTEIN
2 UNITS VEGETABLES
2 UNITS FATS

Baba ghanoush with crunchy vegetables and chicken

SERVES 4 PREP TIME **20 minutes, plus cooling time**
COOKING TIME **50 minutes**

2 carrots, halved and cut into batons
1 red capsicum (pepper), trimmed, seeded and cut into batons
8 baby cos lettuce leaves
2 Lebanese (small) cucumbers, cut into batons
200 g cooked skinless chicken breast, cut into 5 cm strips

BABA GHANOUSH
1 large eggplant (aubergine)
1 large clove garlic, crushed
1 tablespoon tahini
1 tablespoon olive oil
1 tablespoon lemon juice
50 g reduced-fat Greek-style yoghurt

Baba ghanoush (eggplant dip) doesn't normally contain yoghurt, but adding a little makes it extra creamy and delicious.

1 Preheat the oven to 200°C.

2 To make the baba ghanoush, prick the eggplant all over with a fork and place on a small baking tray. Bake for 40–50 minutes or until soft all the way through. Cool for 10 minutes.

3 Halve the eggplant lengthways, then scoop out the flesh into a food processor. Discard the skin. Add the garlic, tahini, oil and lemon juice and process until smooth. Transfer to a bowl and stir in the yoghurt.

4 Arrange the vegetables and chicken on a plate and serve with the baba ghanoush.

1 SERVE =
½ UNIT FRUIT

Mango and pineapple iceblocks

SERVES 6 PREP TIME **10 minutes, plus freezing time**

Sweet frozen fruit is delicious and refreshing on a hot summer's day – these treats will be loved by kids and adults alike. You will need six ⅓ cup (80 ml) popsicle moulds for each of the following recipes.

200 g ripe mango flesh, roughly chopped
1 × 225 g tin pineapple in natural juice
2 teaspoons finely chopped mint

1 Place the mango, pineapple flesh and juice, mint and 100 ml water in a food processor or blender and blend until smooth.
2 Divide among six popsicle moulds, add the sticks and freeze for at least 6 hours or until frozen. Dip briefly in hot water to unmould.

1 SERVE =
½ UNIT FRUIT

Fruity frozen yoghurt iceblocks

SERVES 6 PREP TIME **10 minutes, plus freezing time**

1 ripe banana, mashed
250 g reduced-fat strawberry, peach *or* vanilla yoghurt
1 tablespoon lime juice
100 g small strawberries, cut into 24 thin slices

1 Place the banana, yoghurt and lime juice in a jug and mix until well combined.
2 Carefully arrange four slices of strawberry against the sides of each mould (two on each side), then pour in the yoghurt mixture. Add the sticks and freeze for at least 6 hours or until frozen. Dip briefly in hot water to unmould.

Dinner party or weekend cooking

1 SERVE =

2 UNITS PROTEIN | 1 UNIT VEGETABLES
1 UNIT BREAD | 1 UNIT FATS

Beef, mushroom and red wine stew

SERVES 4 PREP TIME **20 minutes**
COOKING TIME **1 hour 45 minutes**

This is a great dish – once everything is simmering it can be left until the beef is fall-apart tender.

2 teaspoons plain flour
800 g lean beef, cut into 2 cm cubes
1 tablespoon olive oil
1 onion, finely chopped
2 sticks celery, diced
2 cloves garlic, crushed
1 teaspoon dried oregano
1 cup (250 ml) red wine
2 tablespoons tomato paste (puree)
200 g mushrooms, quartered
2 tablespoons chopped flat-leaf parsley
180 g cooked basmati rice (from 80 g uncooked)

1 Combine the flour with 1 teaspoon freshly ground black pepper on a plate. Add the beef cubes and toss to coat.

2 Heat 2 teaspoons of the oil in a flameproof casserole dish or heavy-based saucepan over medium heat. Add the beef in two batches and fry for 3–4 minutes or until golden on all sides. Transfer to a bowl and set aside.

3 Heat the remaining oil in the pan and cook the onion and celery for 4 minutes, then add the garlic and oregano and cook for a further minute. Pour in the wine, then bring to the boil, scraping up the bits from the bottom of the pan.

4 Return the beef to the pan with the tomato paste, mushrooms and 1½ cups (375 ml) water. Bring to the boil, then reduce the heat to low, cover and simmer for 1 hour. After this time, move the lid so it is half-covering the pan, allowing some of the liquid to evaporate, and cook for a further 30 minutes or until the beef is very tender.

5 Stir in the parsley and serve with rice.

1 SERVE =

2 UNITS PROTEIN | 2½ UNITS VEGETABLES
1 UNIT BREAD | 2 UNITS FATS

Baked kingfish with roasted vegetables ›

SERVES 4 PREP TIME **20 minutes**
COOKING TIME **45 minutes**

Kingfish is a rich fish with a firm texture. If you prefer, you could use red snapper, salmon or ling instead.

200 g sweet potato, thinly sliced
1 bulb fennel, trimmed and thinly sliced
400 g pumpkin (squash), peeled and thinly sliced
2 tablespoons olive oil
8 large cloves garlic, unpeeled
250 g roma (plum) tomatoes, on the vine
4 × 200 g kingfish fillets, skin removed and pin-boned
150 g broccolini

1 Preheat the oven to 180°C. Line a large baking tray with baking paper.

2 Arrange the sweet potato, fennel and pumpkin in layers on the baking tray, drizzling each layer with oil and seasoning with freshly ground black pepper. Add the garlic cloves and roast for 20 minutes.

3 Arrange the tomatoes around the outside of the vegetables and bake for a further 10 minutes.

4 Place the fish fillets on top of the vegetables, season with freshly ground black pepper and bake for 10–15 minutes until the fish is just cooked through. Do not overcook or the fish will become dry.

5 Meanwhile, steam the broccolini until tender.

6 Serve the fish on the roast vegetables and steamed broccolini. Season with a final grinding of pepper, then squeeze the soft flesh from each garlic clove over the top.

TIP Wedges of onion can be included with the vegetables, if you like.

1 SERVE =
1½ UNITS PROTEIN
1 UNIT BREAD
1 UNIT DAIRY
½ UNIT VEGETABLES
½ UNIT FATS

Fish pie

SERVES 6 PREP TIME **25 minutes, plus standing time**
COOKING TIME **50 minutes**

4 eggs
200 g desiree potatoes, roughly chopped
1 × 400 g tin cannellini beans, rinsed and drained
600 ml reduced-fat milk
3 tablespoons reduced-fat olive oil spread
2½ tablespoons plain flour
½ cup (60 g) grated reduced-fat cheddar
2 tablespoons chopped flat-leaf parsley
400 g flathead fillet, skin removed and pin-boned, cut into 3 cm pieces
400 g salmon fillet, skin removed and pin-boned, cut into 3 cm pieces
200 g raw peeled prawns, cut into three pieces
100 g frozen peas, thawed

Fish pie is a welcome sight on a cold winter's evening. Here the pie topping has been made low-GI by combining cannellini beans with the potato. Buy ready-peeled prawns from the supermarket to save time.

1 Preheat the oven to 180°C.

2 Carefully put the eggs into a pan of simmering water and cook for 7 minutes. Remove and plunge into cold water. Once cold, peel and roughly chop.

3 Meanwhile, cook the potato in boiling water until tender. Drain well, then return to the pan. Add the cannellini beans and 2 tablespoons of the milk. Mash until very smooth, adding extra milk if necessary. Season with freshly ground black pepper.

4 Melt the reduced-fat spread in a small saucepan over low–medium heat. Stir in the flour and mix until well combined. Cook, without browning, for 1 minute, stirring regularly. Whisking continuously, gradually add the remaining milk, whisking well after each addition to prevent lumps forming. Once all the milk has been incorporated and the sauce is smooth, add the cheese and stir until melted. Cook for a further 2 minutes, then stir in the parsley and set aside.

5 Place the fish, prawns and peas in a 1 litre capacity baking dish or six 1 cup (250 ml) ovenproof dishes. Pour the sauce over and mix gently. Scatter with the chopped egg, then spoon over the mash topping, covering the fish mixture entirely. Place on a baking tray and bake for 20–30 minutes or until the fish is cooked through.

6 Leave to stand for 5 minutes before serving.

1 SERVE =
2 UNITS PROTEIN
1¼ UNITS BREAD
¼ UNIT DAIRY
2 UNITS VEGETABLES
1 UNIT FATS

Harissa and yoghurt marinated salmon with herbed vegetables

SERVES 4 PREP TIME **20 minutes, plus marinating time**
COOKING TIME **10 minutes**

1½ tablespoons harissa paste
100 g reduced-fat Greek-style yoghurt
1 tablespoon lemon juice
1 tablespoon chopped coriander
800 g salmon fillets, skin removed and pin-boned
cooking oil spray
180 g cooked basmati rice (from 80 g uncooked)
lemon wedges, to serve

HERBED VEGETABLES
2 bunches asparagus, trimmed and cut into 3 cm lengths
100 g frozen peas
300 g green beans, trimmed and cut into 3 cm lengths
2 teaspoons olive oil
1 tablespoon chopped flat-leaf parsley

Marinating the salmon gives it an added depth of flavour. The yoghurt considerably calms the heat of the chilli in the harissa, but if it still seems like too much harissa for your liking, just reduce the quantity to suit your taste.

1 Combine the harissa, yoghurt, lemon juice and coriander. Place the salmon fillets in a shallow dish and spoon over the marinade. Rub all over to coat the fish, then cover and leave to marinate in the fridge for at least 30 minutes and up to 8 hours.

2 Spray a chargrill pan with cooking oil and preheat over medium–high heat. Scrape any excess marinade from the salmon and cook for 3–4 minutes on each side or until just cooked through; the exact cooking time will depend on the thickness of the fish. Do not overcook or the fish will become dry.

3 Meanwhile, to make the herbed vegetables, steam the asparagus, peas and beans for 4–5 minutes until tender, then transfer to a serving dish. Drizzle over the oil, add the parsley and season with plenty of freshly ground black pepper. Toss to combine.

4 Serve the fish with the rice, herbed vegetables and lemon wedges for squeezing over.

1 SERVE =
2 UNITS PROTEIN
1 UNIT BREAD
2 UNITS VEGETABLES
½ UNIT FATS

Seafood stew

SERVES 4 PREP TIME **25 minutes** COOKING TIME **20 minutes**

4 firm, ripe tomatoes
2 teaspoons olive oil
1 onion, chopped
1 bulb fennel, trimmed, halved and sliced
1 teaspoon dried oregano
½ cup (125 ml) dry white wine
1 bay leaf
200 g salmon fillet, skin removed and pin-boned, cut into 2 cm pieces
200 g ling or other firm white fish fillet, skin removed and pin-boned, cut into 2 cm pieces
200 g raw peeled prawns
200 g black mussels, scrubbed and debearded
180 g cooked basmati rice (from 80 g uncooked)
lemon wedges, to serve

This wonderfully satisfying stew is inspired by the flavours of the Mediterranean: fennel, oregano and fresh seafood. Buy ready-peeled prawns from the supermarket to save time.

1 Cut a shallow cross into the base of each tomato. Place the tomatoes in a bowl of boiling water for 30 seconds, then plunge into cold water for 10 seconds. Remove and peel off the skin, starting from the cross. Quarter and remove the seeds, then roughly chop the flesh. Set aside.

2 Heat the oil in a flameproof casserole dish over low–medium heat. Add the onion and fennel and cook for 10 minutes or until softened, stirring occasionally. Increase the heat to high, add the oregano and wine and allow it to boil for a few minutes.

3 Add the bay leaf, chopped tomato and 1 cup (250 ml) water and bring to the boil. Add the fish and cook for 3 minutes. Add the prawns and mussels, then stir gently and cook for 3–4 minutes or until the prawns have turned pink and are cooked through and the mussels have opened. (Discard any mussels that do not open).

4 Serve the seafood stew with basmati rice and lemon wedges for squeezing over the top.

1 SERVE =
2 UNITS PROTEIN
2 UNITS VEGETABLES
½ UNIT FATS

French-style chicken and mushroom casserole

SERVES 4 PREP TIME **20 minutes, plus soaking time**
COOKING TIME **50 minutes**

15 g dried cep (porcini) *or* 100 g small Swiss brown mushrooms
4 firm, ripe tomatoes
6 sprigs thyme
1 bay leaf
2 teaspoons olive oil
1 kg skinless chicken pieces, on the bone
8 red or golden shallots
3 cloves garlic, crushed
1 cup (250 ml) dry white wine
2 tablespoons chopped flat-leaf parsley (optional)
300 g steamed green beans

Cep (or porcini) are wild mushrooms with a rich, sweet, nutty flavour. When dried, the flavour becomes more intense, so a few go a long way. If you can't find cep, small brown mushrooms will also add a lovely flavour to this casserole.

1 If using cep mushrooms, soak them in 150 ml hot water for 20 minutes. Drain, reserving the soaking liquid.

2 Meanwhile, cut a shallow cross into the base of each tomato. Place the tomatoes in a bowl of boiling water for 30 seconds, then plunge into cold water for 10 seconds. Remove and peel off the skin, starting from the cross. Quarter and remove the seeds, then roughly chop the flesh. Set aside.

3 Tie the thyme and bay leaf together with kitchen string.

4 Heat the oil in a flameproof casserole dish or heavy-based saucepan over medium heat. Working in batches, lightly brown the chicken for 3–4 minutes, turning regularly, then transfer to a plate.

5 Add the shallots to the pan and cook for 5 minutes. Add the garlic and cook for 1 minute. Return the chicken to the pan with the chopped tomato, herbs, wine and mushroom soaking liquid. Season well with freshly ground black pepper. Cover and bring to the boil, then reduce the heat and simmer for 30 minutes or until the chicken is cooked through .

6 Add the mushrooms and cook, uncovered, for 3–4 minutes. Remove the thyme and bay leaf, and sprinkle with parsley, if you like. Serve with steamed green beans.

1 SERVE =
2 UNITS PROTEIN
1 UNIT BREAD
3 UNITS VEGETABLES
2 UNITS FATS

Spice-rubbed pot roast beef with celeriac mash

SERVES 4 PREP TIME **20 minutes, plus resting time**
COOKING TIME **30 minutes**

800 g beef fillet
2 tablespoons olive oil
2 cloves garlic, crushed
1 teaspoon ground cardamom
2 teaspoons ground coriander
1 large onion, halved and thinly sliced
½ cup (125 ml) red wine
1 × 400 g tin chopped tomatoes
150 g steamed green beans

CELERIAC MASH
1 celeriac, peeled and chopped
360 g potato, roughly chopped
2 tablespoons reduced-fat milk

This is a simple yet sophisticated dish to cook for a dinner party – just be careful not to overcook the beef.

1 Trim any excess fat from the beef fillet, then remove any membrane by sliding a sharp knife between the meat and the membrane. If the fillet tapers, fold the thinner end under the thicker part to form an even thickness – this will help it to cook evenly.

2 Combine 1 tablespoon of the oil with the garlic, cardamom, coriander and 1 teaspoon freshly ground black pepper in a small bowl. Rub all over the beef.

3 Preheat the oven to 180°C.

4 Heat 3 teaspoons of the oil in a flameproof casserole dish over medium heat. Add the beef and cook, turning, for 6 minutes or until golden brown on all sides. Remove to a plate.

5 Reduce the heat to low, then add the remaining oil and cook the onion for 5 minutes. Pour in the red wine and scrape up any bits from the bottom of the pan. Stir in the tomato, then return the beef to the pan and spoon over a little of the tomato sauce. Cover and bring to the boil, then transfer to the oven and roast for 15 minutes or until rare (or 20 minutes for medium–rare). Remove from the oven and leave to rest for 15 minutes.

6 Meanwhile, to make the celeriac mash, place the celeriac and potato in a saucepan and just cover with water. Bring to the boil, then reduce the heat to low and simmer for 20 minutes or until the celeriac is very soft. Drain well, then return the pan to low heat to evaporate any excess water. Add the milk and use a stick blender or potato masher to form a smooth puree.

7 Cut the beef into thick slices and serve with the tomato sauce, celeriac mash and green beans.

1 SERVE =
2 UNITS PROTEIN
½ UNIT BREAD
¼ UNIT DAIRY
1½ UNITS VEGETABLES
1½ UNITS FATS

Chicken and vegetable pie

SERVES 4 PREP TIME **30 minutes, plus standing time**
COOKING TIME **35 minutes**

2 teaspoons olive oil
1 onion, chopped
1 leek, trimmed, white part only, washed and thinly sliced
1 red capsicum (pepper), trimmed, seeded and diced
200 g mushrooms, chopped
1 tablespoon plain flour
60 g reduced-fat cream cheese
150 ml reduced-fat milk
2 tablespoons snipped chives
800 g cooked skinless chicken breast, shredded
cooking oil spray
4 sheets filo pastry, halved

Using filo rather than shortcrust or puff pastry significantly reduces the amount of fat in this chicken pie, so you can relax and enjoy it.

1 Heat the oil in a large heavy-based saucepan. Add the onion, leek and capsicum and cook for 8–10 minutes until softened. Add the mushroom and cook for 3–4 minutes. Sprinkle over the flour and stir with a wooden spoon, scraping up any bits from the bottom. Cook for 1 minute.

2 Add the cream cheese and stir well. Gradually add the milk, stirring well after each addition, until the mixture thickens. Add the chives and season well with freshly ground black pepper. Remove from the heat and stir in the chicken.

3 Preheat the oven to 180°C. Spray a 1 litre capacity pie dish with cooking oil.

4 Place a half-piece of filo pastry on a clean work surface and spray lightly with cooking oil. Put it into the pie dish so it covers just over half the dish, allowing the excess to hang over the edge. Repeat with a second piece of filo, lining the other side of the dish. Turn the dish a quarter turn and repeat with two more pieces of filo. Repeat this process with the remaining filo until all the sheets are used. Spoon the chicken filling into the pastry case and smooth the top. Fold the overhanging pastry back over to cover the filling.

5 Bake for 15 minutes or until the pastry is golden brown. Leave to stand for 5 minutes, then cut the pie into wedges and serve.

1 SERVE =
2 UNITS PROTEIN
1 UNIT BREAD
½ UNIT DAIRY
1½ UNIT VEGETABLES
1½ UNITS FATS

Indian lamb curry with minted green beans

SERVES 4 PREP TIME **20 minutes** COOKING TIME **1 hour 50 minutes**

1 tablespoon olive oil
800 g boned lamb shoulder or leg, trimmed of fat and diced
6 cardamom pods
6 cloves
1 cinnamon stick
2 onions, chopped
1 × 5 cm piece ginger, finely grated
2 cloves garlic, crushed
1 teaspoon ground coriander
1 teaspoon ground cumin
1 teaspoon hot paprika
½ teaspoon chilli powder
100 g reduced-fat Greek-style yoghurt
180 g cooked basmati rice (from 80 g uncooked)

MINTED GREEN BEANS
300 g green beans, trimmed and cut into 4 cm lengths
2 teaspoons olive oil
1 green chilli, thinly sliced
2 tablespoons chopped mint

The whole spices in this recipe will need to be removed before serving. The minted green beans add a deliciously fresh contrast.

1 Heat 2 teaspoons of the oil in a large flameproof casserole dish or heavy-based saucepan over medium heat. Add the lamb in batches and cook for 3–4 minutes or until brown all over, stirring occasionally. Remove from the pan with a slotted spoon and set aside. Add the cardamom pods, cloves and cinnamon stick and cook for 30 seconds, then add the onion and cook for 5 minutes, stirring regularly.

2 Add the ginger and garlic and cook for 30 seconds, then stir in the ground spices and cook for 1 minute. Return the meat and any juices to the pan and stir to coat. Add 1 tablespoon of the yoghurt and stir until well combined. Gradually stir in the remaining yoghurt until well combined. Cook, stirring, for 3–4 minutes.

3 Pour in 300 ml water and bring to the boil, scraping any bits off the base and side of the pan. Reduce the heat to very low and simmer, covered, for 1¼–1½ hours or until the lamb is very tender, stirring every 10 minutes or so. Once cooked, remove and discard the whole spices.

4 Meanwhile, to make the minted green beans, steam the beans until tender. Heat the oil in a frying pan, add the chilli and stir-fry for 1 minute. Remove the pan from the heat, add the beans and mint and toss well to combine.

5 Serve the curry with basmati rice and the minted green beans.

1 SERVE =
2 UNITS PROTEIN
1 UNIT BREAD
2½ UNITS VEGETABLES
1 UNIT FATS

Moroccan lamb stew with vegetable couscous

SERVES 4 PREP TIME **20 minutes** COOKING TIME **1 hour 30 minutes**

2 teaspoons olive oil
800 g lamb leg or fillet, trimmed of fat, cubed
1 red onion, halved and sliced
2 cloves garlic, crushed
small pinch saffron threads
1 teaspoon ground coriander
1 teaspoon ground cumin
½ teaspoon ground ginger
1 × 400 g tin chopped tomatoes
3 small thin eggplants (aubergines), halved lengthways and cut into 2 cm pieces
2 tablespoons chopped coriander (optional)

VEGETABLE COUSCOUS
60 g couscous
2 teaspoons olive oil
100 g frozen peas
16 green beans, trimmed and cut into 2 cm lengths
2 tablespoons chopped coriander

This aromatic, hearty stew becomes even more delicious if left for a few hours for the flavours to develop. If you can, cook the stew in the morning and leave it to cool, then refrigerate and reheat it in the evening, while you prepare the couscous.

1 Heat the oil in a flameproof casserole dish or heavy-based saucepan over medium heat. Add the lamb in two batches and cook for 3–4 minutes or until browned all over, stirring occasionally. Remove to a plate. Add the onion and garlic and cook for 5 minutes, then stir in the spices and cook for 1 minute.

2 Add the tomato and 1 cup (250 ml) water. Cover and bring to the boil, then reduce the heat to low and simmer for 1 hour. Add the eggplant, pushing it down into the sauce, then replace the lid so it is half-covering the pan, allowing some of the liquid to evaporate. Cook for a further 15 minutes or until the eggplant is tender. If the stew is still quite liquidy, remove the lid and cook for a further 5 minutes until reduced.

3 Meanwhile, to make the vegetable couscous, bring 100 ml water to the boil in a small saucepan. Add the couscous and oil, then fork through the grains to separate them. Remove the pan from the heat, cover and leave to stand for 2 minutes. Return to a very low heat and cook for 3 minutes, continuing to fork through the grains. Remove from the heat and stir the grains gently.

4 Blanch the peas and beans, then drain. Add to the couscous with the coriander and mix well.

5 Stir the coriander (if using) into the lamb stew and serve with the vegetable couscous.

1 SERVE =
2 UNITS PROTEIN
1 UNIT BREAD
1½ UNITS VEGETABLES
½ UNIT FATS

Teriyaki pork with stir-fried greens

SERVES 4 PREP TIME **20 minutes, plus marinating and resting time**
COOKING TIME **20 minutes**

3 tablespoons salt-reduced soy sauce
2 tablespoons mirin
2 teaspoons honey
2 cloves garlic, crushed
1 × 5 cm piece ginger, finely grated
800 g pork loin fillet, trimmed of fat
cooking oil spray
180 g cooked basmati rice (from 80 g uncooked)

STIR-FRIED GREENS
1 teaspoon sesame seeds
1 tablespoon salt-reduced soy sauce
1 tablespoon rice wine vinegar
1 teaspoon vegetable oil
1 teaspoon sesame oil
1 bunch bok choy, leaves separated and washed, roughly chopped
200 g snowpeas (mange-tout), sliced in half on an angle
1 bunch spinach, washed, tough stalks discarded

It's important not to overcook pork, otherwise it will become dry. Serving it a little pink in the middle keeps it moist and succulent.

1 Combine the soy sauce, mirin, honey, garlic, ginger and 1 teaspoon freshly ground black pepper in a small bowl. Make a few shallow cuts across the pork loin and place in a shallow dish. Pour over the marinade and rub it into the cuts. Cover and set aside to marinate for at least 30 minutes and up to 12 hours.

2 Preheat the oven to 180°C and place a baking dish in the oven to heat up.

3 Remove the pork from the marinade and pat dry. Heat a frying pan or chargrill pan over medium heat and spray lightly with cooking oil. Cook the pork for 10 minutes, turning regularly.

4 Transfer the pork to the baking dish in the oven and roast for 10 minutes. Remove from the oven, wrap in foil and leave to rest for 10 minutes. The pork will continue to cook, so this resting time is important; the pork should be slightly pink in the middle at this point, but if you prefer, leave it to rest for a further 5 minutes.

5 Meanwhile, to make the stir-fried greens, heat a small frying pan over medium heat and toast the sesame seeds for 1–2 minutes or until golden, shaking the pan regularly. Transfer to a small bowl and set aside.

6 Combine the soy sauce and rice vinegar in a small bowl. Heat the vegetable and sesame oils in a wok over medium–high heat. Add the bok choy and stir-fry for 1 minute. Add the snowpeas and spinach and stir-fry for 1 minute. Pour in the soy sauce mixture and stir-fry for 1 minute. Scatter the sesame seeds over the top.

7 Cut the pork into thick slices and serve with the stir-fried greens and basmati rice.

1 SERVE =
½ UNIT PROTEIN
1½ UNITS BREAD
1 UNIT DAIRY
2 UNITS VEGETABLES
1 UNIT FATS

Roasted capsicum and feta filo tart

SERVES 4 PREP TIME **30 minutes, plus standing time**
COOKING TIME **55 minutes**

1 tablespoon olive oil
3 red capsicums (peppers), trimmed, seeded and cut into 3 cm pieces
2 leeks, trimmed, white part only, washed and thinly sliced
2 cloves garlic, crushed
180 g cooked basmati rice (from 80 g uncooked)
2 teaspoons capers, rinsed and finely chopped
80 g reduced-fat feta, crumbled
2 tablespoons chopped basil
2 eggs, lightly beaten
4 sheets filo pastry, halved
cooking oil spray
150 g mixed salad leaves

This is delicious as a weekend lunch.

1 Preheat the oven to 180°C.

2 Pour 2 teaspoons of the oil into a roasting tin and place it in the oven. Once the oil is hot, add the capsicum, season with freshly ground black pepper and toss so the capsicum is well coated in the oil and pepper. Roast for 40 minutes or until soft, shaking the tin occasionally.

3 Meanwhile, heat the remaining oil in a large frying pan over medium heat. Add the leek and cook, covered, for 10 minutes, stirring regularly. Add the garlic and cook for 2 minutes. Transfer to a large bowl and stir in the cooked rice, capers, feta, basil and beaten egg.

4 Spray half a sheet of filo pastry very lightly with cooking oil and lay a second sheet on top at a 90 degree angle. Spray again, then continue to layer the pastry, spraying and turning each new sheet at an angle. Carefully place in a 1 litre capacity baking dish or 20 cm tart tin with a removable base, pushing the pastry into the sides.

5 Add the roasted capsicum to the filling and mix well. Carefully tip into the pastry case, smooth the top and bake for 15 minutes or until the pastry is golden. Leave to stand for 5 minutes, then serve with mixed salad leaves.

1 SERVE =
2 UNITS PROTEIN
½ UNIT BREAD
1½ UNITS VEGETABLES
2 UNITS FATS

Balsamic-glazed lamb fillet with sage, sweet potato and leek

SERVES 4 PREP TIME **20 minutes, plus resting time**
COOKING TIME **25 minutes**

1 tablespoon olive oil
200 g sweet potato, cut into 1.5 cm cubes
3 large leeks, white part only, trimmed, washed and thinly sliced
150 g broccolini, cut into 4 cm lengths
1 tablespoon finely chopped sage, plus extra leaves to garnish

BALSAMIC-GLAZED LAMB
½ cup (125 ml) balsamic vinegar
2 cloves garlic, crushed
800 g lamb fillet, trimmed of fat
1 tablespoon olive oil

Cooking the leeks slowly not only develops their flavour, it also gives them a lovely, melt-in-the-mouth softness.

1 Preheat the oven to 180°C.

2 Pour 2 teaspoons of the oil into a small baking dish and place it in the oven to heat up. Once the oil is hot, add the sweet potato, season with freshly ground black pepper and toss so the sweet potato is well coated in the oil and pepper. Roast for 20 minutes or until softened, shaking the dish occasionally.

3 Heat the remaining oil in a large frying pan over low heat. Add the leek and cook, covered, for 20 minutes or until really soft, stirring occasionally. Uncover, increase the heat slightly and cook for a further 2 minutes. Remove from the heat and stir in the chopped sage and roast sweet potato.

4 Meanwhile, to make the balsamic-glazed lamb, place the vinegar and garlic in a small saucepan, along with a generous grinding of freshly ground black pepper. Bring to the boil, then reduce the heat to low and simmer for 10 minutes or until thickened and syrupy. Set aside in the pan.

5 Preheat a chargrill pan over medium heat. Brush the lamb fillet with the oil, then chargrill on all sides for 8 minutes. Brush the balsamic reduction all over the lamb (reserving any left over), then transfer to a baking tray and roast at 180°C for 5 minutes for medium–rare (or 10 minutes for medium). Remove from the oven, cover with foil and leave to rest for 5 minutes – the lamb will continue to cook during this time.

6 Steam the broccolini until tender.

7 Briefly reheat the remaining balsamic glaze in the pan. Cut the lamb into thick slices and serve with the broccolini, sweet potato and leek. Finish with a drizzle of the balsamic glaze and a scattering of extra sage leaves.

1 SERVE =
2 UNITS PROTEIN
1 UNIT BREAD
1½ UNITS VEGETABLES
2 UNITS FATS

Chicken and vegetable pilaf

SERVES 4 PREP TIME **25 minutes, plus standing time**
COOKING TIME **50 minutes**

This is a great combination of flavours and textures: soft, tender basmati rice, fresh vegetables and chicken, topped off with crunchy almonds.

- **1 tablespoon olive oil**
- **1 onion, halved and thinly sliced**
- **2 sticks celery, finely chopped**
- **1 leek, white part only, trimmed, washed and thinly sliced**
- **2 cinnamon sticks**
- **6 cloves**
- **2 cloves garlic, crushed**
- **1 teaspoon ground coriander**
- **1 teaspoon ground cumin**
- **800 g skinless chicken breast fillet, cut into thin strips**
- **200 g button mushrooms, halved or quartered**
- **2 zucchinis (courgettes), halved lengthways and thickly sliced**
- **80 g basmati rice**
- **1 × 400 g tin chopped tomatoes**
- **40 g slivered almonds**
- **coriander sprigs and lemon wedges, to serve (optional)**

1. Heat the oil in a large heavy-based frying pan or flameproof casserole dish. Add the onion, celery and leek and cook over low-medium heat for 10 minutes. Add the cinnamon, cloves and garlic and cook for 1 minute. Stir in the ground spices and chicken and cook for 5 minutes.
2. Add the mushrooms, zucchini and rice and cook for 2 minutes, stirring regularly. Add the tomatoes and 1 cup (250 ml) water and season well with freshly ground black pepper. Stir everything around to mix well, then bring to the boil. Smooth the top, then reduce the heat to low and cook, covered, for 20 minutes or until the rice is tender and most of the liquid has been absorbed. Stir occasionally, smoothing the top each time. Increase the heat to medium, then remove the lid and cook for a further 5 minutes to evaporate some of the remaining liquid. Remove from the heat and leave to stand for 5 minutes, covered.
3. Meanwhile, heat a small frying pan over medium heat and toast the almonds for 1–2 minutes or until golden, shaking the pan regularly. Set aside.
4. Scatter the almonds and coriander sprigs (if using) over the pilaf and serve with lemon wedges to squeeze over, if you like.

TIP If you like a bit of heat, add ½–1 small red chilli, seeded and finely chopped, when you add the garlic.

1 SERVE =
2 UNITS PROTEIN
1 UNIT BREAD
1½ UNITS DAIRY
1½ UNITS VEGETABLES
1½ UNITS FATS

Polenta pizza triangles with grilled chicken

SERVES 4 PREP TIME **30 minutes, plus cooling and standing time**
COOKING TIME **40 minutes**

These colourful triangles of polenta are a healthier alternative to traditional pizza dough, and the parmesan adds a good depth of flavour. It's best to use a 20 cm square baking dish to ensure the polenta is the right thickness.

cooking oil spray
2 teaspoons olive oil
1 tablespoon balsamic vinegar
800 g skinless chicken breast fillet
50 g wild rocket
100 g cherry tomatoes, quartered
80 g avocado, diced
80 g reduced-fat feta, crumbled
small handful small basil leaves (optional)

POLENTA PIZZA TRIANGLES
2 cups (500 ml) salt-reduced chicken stock
80 g polenta
1 tablespoon finely grated parmesan

1 Preheat the oven to 180°C. Spray a 20 cm square baking dish with cooking oil.

2 To make the polenta pizza triangles, bring the stock to the boil in a saucepan. Add the polenta in a slow, steady steam, stirring constantly. Reduce the heat to low and continue to stir for 10 minutes or until the grains are soft and bright yellow. Remove from the heat and stir in the parmesan until melted. Quickly spoon into the baking dish and smooth the top. Bake for 15 minutes, then remove and leave to cool completely in the dish.

3 Meanwhile, combine the oil and 2 teaspoons of the vinegar in a small bowl and season with freshly ground black pepper. Cut the chicken breasts in half widthways through the centre to form thin slices. Brush the marinade all over the chicken and set aside for 20 minutes.

4 Run a knife around the edge of the cooled polenta, then turn out onto a board. Cut into four squares, then cut each square in half on the diagonal to form two triangles.

5 Preheat the oven grill to high and line the grill tray with foil. Grill the triangles, soft-side up, for 5 minutes or until starting to brown around the edges. Remove and keep warm, then grill the chicken for 10 minutes or until cooked through, turning regularly.

6 Toss the rocket in the remaining vinegar and season with freshly ground black pepper.

7 To serve, top the polenta triangles with the dressed rocket, tomato, avocado and feta and garnish with basil leaves, if you like. Thickly slice the chicken and serve with the polenta pizzas.

1 SERVE =
2 UNITS PROTEIN
1 UNIT BREAD
3 UNITS VEGETABLES
1 UNIT FATS

Warm silken tofu with Asian vegetables

SERVES 4 PREP TIME **20 minutes** COOKING TIME **15 minutes**

2 teaspoons sesame seeds
800 g silken tofu
2 tablespoons salt-reduced soy sauce
2 tablespoons rice wine vinegar
1 teaspoon sesame oil
1 teaspoon finely grated ginger
300 g mixed Asian mushrooms, such as shiitake, enoki and oyster
2 teaspoons vegetable oil
1 bunch bok choy, washed, trimmed and cut into eight thin wedges
200 g snowpeas (mange-tout), sliced in half on an angle
1 bunch spinach, washed, tough stalks discarded
180 g cooked basmati rice (from 80 g uncooked)
3 spring onions, white part only, thinly sliced on the diagonal

Silken tofu has a wonderful, soft texture. When steamed in a marinade, it soaks up the flavours as it cooks. The marinade is also delicious served over the vegetables.

1 Heat a small frying pan over medium heat and toast the sesame seeds for 1–2 minutes or until golden, shaking the pan regularly. Transfer to a small bowl and set aside.

2 Pat the tofu dry with paper towel. Place in a heatproof bowl or shallow dish with a lip that will fit inside a steamer. Combine the soy sauce, vinegar, sesame oil, ginger and 2 tablespoons water and pour over the tofu. Steam for 6 minutes, carefully spooning the marinade over the tofu twice while it is steaming. Set the bowl of tofu aside.

3 Trim and discard the bottom 3 cm from the enoki mushrooms (if using). Roughly chop the remaining mushrooms, keeping the enoki mushrooms separate.

4 Heat the vegetable oil in a wok or large frying pan over medium–high heat. Add the bok choy and stir-fry for 2 minutes, carefully adding 1–2 tablespoons water while cooking. Add the snowpeas and mushrooms (except the enoki) and stir-fry for 1 minute. Add the spinach and enoki and stir-fry for 2 minutes or until the spinach has wilted.

5 Leaving the tofu in the bowl it was steamed in, carefully cut it into large cubes.

6 Divide the basmati rice among four bowls, then top with the tofu and vegetables and spoon over the marinade. Scatter with spring onion and sesame seeds and serve.

Desserts

1 SERVE =
1 UNIT BREAD
½ UNIT DAIRY
1 UNIT FRUIT
2 UNITS FATS

Fruit crumble with orange yoghurt

SERVES 4 PREP TIME **25 minutes** COOKING TIME **35 minutes**

finely grated zest and juice of 1 orange
1 apple, peeled and diced
2 firm, ripe pears, peeled, cored and diced
120 g frozen blackberries, raspberries or mixed berries
½ cup (45 g) rolled oats (not the instant variety)
1½ tablespoons wholemeal plain flour
1 tablespoon reduced-fat olive oil spread
1 tablespoon Splenda
20 g pistachios, roughly chopped
20 g almonds, roughly chopped
400 g reduced-fat Greek-style yoghurt

Once you've tried this dessert it's sure to become a firm favourite. Use whatever fruit you have to hand: try fresh berries, rhubarb, or apple and pear.

1 Preheat the oven to 170°C.

2 Reserve 1 tablespoon of the orange juice, then place the remaining juice in a small saucepan with the apple. Cover and cook over medium heat for 5 minutes. Transfer the apple and any cooking juices to a 1 litre capacity baking dish and stir in the pear and berries. (You could also make individual crumbles in four 1 cup [250 ml] ovenproof dishes, if you prefer.)

3 Meanwhile, place half the rolled oats in a blender and process for 2 minutes until finely chopped. Transfer to a bowl along with the remaining oats and sift in the flour, returning the husks to the bowl. Add the reduced-fat spread and mix thoroughly with your fingers until it feels like each grain is coated in the spread. Stir in the Splenda and nuts.

4 Spoon the crumble topping over the fruit and bake for 30 minutes or until the top is golden.

5 Combine the yoghurt, orange zest and reserved juice in a small serving dish.

6 Leave the crumble to stand for 5 minutes, then serve with the orange yoghurt.

1 SERVE =
½ UNIT DAIRY
¾ UNIT FRUIT

‹ Berry and ginger compote

SERVES 4 PREP TIME **20 minutes, plus cooling time**
COOKING TIME **12 minutes**

These scrumptious pots of juicy berries are delicious served warm or cold.

finely grated zest of 1 lemon, plus 1 tablespoon juice
400 g reduced-fat Greek-style yoghurt
450 g mixed berries, larger berries chopped
2 teaspoons finely grated ginger
1 stalk lemongrass, white part only, bruised

1 Stir the lemon zest into the yoghurt and set aside.

2 Cut a disc of baking paper the same diameter as the saucepan to be used to cook the fruit. Place the berries, ginger, lemongrass and 1½ tablespoons water in the saucepan, tucking the lemongrass around the fruit. Cook over low–medium heat until the mixture starts to simmer. Press the paper disc down gently over the mixture to cover, then place the lid on and simmer for 10 minutes or until the berries are soft but still retain their shape. Remove from the heat.

3 Leave the berries to cool to room temperature, then remove the lemongrass and stir in the lemon juice.

4 Spoon the fruit into four small glasses, then top with the lemon yoghurt. Serve warm, or chill until needed.

1 SERVE =
¾ UNIT FRUIT

Watermelon granita

SERVES 4 PREP TIME **15 minutes, plus freezing time**

To achieve the delicious icy crystals of a granita, it's important to keep scraping the mixture while it is freezing. If you don't do this, the result will be a block of frozen watermelon ice.

½ cup (15 g) Splenda
450 g trimmed seedless watermelon, roughly chopped
finely grated zest and juice of 1 orange
1 teaspoon finely grated ginger

1 Dissolve the Splenda in ¾ cup (185 ml) water. Pour into a food processor, add the remaining ingredients and pulse briefly until the watermelon is well chopped but not pureed or mushy. Transfer to a shallow metal tray (about 1.25–1.5 litre capacity) and freeze for 2½ hours or until the mixture is starting to freeze around the edges.

2 Scrape the frozen edges back into the mixture with a fork and stir around, then return the tray to the freezer. Repeat this every 30 minutes for 3 hours, then leave to freeze completely.

3 Scrape the watermelon granita into small bowls and serve.

1 SERVE =
¾ UNIT DAIRY
½ UNIT FRUIT

Tangy vanilla panna cotta

SERVES 6 PREP TIME **25 minutes, plus standing and refrigerating time**
COOKING TIME **3 minutes**

1 tablespoon powdered gelatine
1 cup (250 ml) reduced-fat milk
2 teaspoons vanilla essence or 1 teaspoon vanilla extract
finely grated zest of 2 lemons
600 g reduced-fat Greek-style yoghurt
½ cup (15 g) Splenda
300 g raspberries, to serve

Serve these creamy mounds of lemony vanilla panna cotta surrounded by fresh raspberries – the perfect end to a meal.

1 Place 3 tablespoons hot water in a small bowl, sprinkle over the gelatine and leave for 1 minute until it becomes spongy. Stir briskly with a fork until the gelatine dissolves, then set aside.

2 Heat the milk until hot but not boiling. Add the gelatine mixture and whisk until it dissolves. Stir in the vanilla and lemon zest and set aside for 5 minutes.

3 Beat together the yoghurt and Splenda until well combined. Stir in the milk mixture and whisk until well combined. Pour into six 150 ml glasses or moulds and tap each one on the work surface to remove any air bubbles. Cover with plastic film and chill in the fridge for 1–2 hours until set.

4 Run a knife around the outside of the glasses or moulds and turn out the panna cotta onto serving plates. (Alternatively, serve them in their containers.) Scatter a few raspberries around the plate and serve.

TIPS

These can be made up to 24 hours in advance.

If you like things extra lemony, add 1 tablespoon lemon juice to the mixture when the lemon zest is added.

1 SERVE =
½ UNIT DAIRY

Chocolate pots

SERVES 4 PREP TIME **15 minutes, plus refrigerating time**

3 tablespoons Splenda
1½ tablespoons cocoa powder, plus extra for dusting
½ cup (125 ml) boiling water
2 teaspoons powdered gelatine
1 x 375 ml tin reduced-fat evaporated milk

These chocolate pots are lovely and light with a smooth, silky texture, so you can indulge your chocolate cravings guilt-free.

1 Combine the Splenda, cocoa powder and 2 tablespoons of the boiling water in a small heatproof bowl and blend until smooth.

2 In another small heatproof bowl, combine the remaining boiling water with the gelatine and leave for 1 minute until it becomes spongy. Stir briskly with a fork until the gelatine dissolves, then set aside to cool for 5 minutes. Stir in the cocoa mixture.

3 Place the evaporated milk in a large bowl and beat with electric beaters for 1–2 minutes or until light and fluffy. Fold in the cocoa mixture with a metal spoon, mixing it until smooth. Transfer the mixture to a jug and stir to combine.

4 Immediately pour the mixture through a fine-meshed sieve into four ½ cup (125 ml) capacity serving pots or glasses. Cover with plastic film and chill in the fridge for 4–5 hours until set.

5 Dust with extra cocoa powder and serve.

1 SERVE =
½ UNIT DAIRY
1 UNIT FRUIT

Pineapple and mint crush with lime 'ice-cream'

SERVES 4 PREP TIME **20 minutes, plus freezing and refrigerating time**

400 g reduced-fat Greek-style yoghurt
finely grated zest and juice of 1 lime
600 g pineapple flesh, diced
1 tablespoon finely chopped mint, plus extra small mint leaves to serve

This dessert is quick and easy to prepare, and nothing says summer quite like the tropical flavours of pineapple and lime.

1. Combine the yoghurt with the lime zest and juice. Mix well, then place in the freezer for 4 hours or until semi-frozen.
2. Meanwhile, place the pineapple in a bowl and stir in the mint. Chill in the fridge, then place in the freezer for 20–30 minutes before serving.
3. To serve, divide the frosted pineapple among four serving bowls and add a scoop of lime 'ice-cream', then scatter with small mint leaves.

About the authors

Professor Peter Clifton A high-profile clinical and nutrition researcher for more than 20 years, he joined Baker IDI in July 2009. While he was at CSIRO, he co-authored *The CSIRO Total Wellbeing Diet* books. His primary research interest is the use of diet in the prevention and treatment of cardiovascular disease and its risk factors: obesity and diabetes. Peter has a clinical practice specialising in lipid management at the Flinders Medical Centre, and in diabetes and cardiovascular disease at the Royal Adelaide Hospital. He has written articles for newspapers and medical magazines, discussion papers for food companies and books for the public. He is on the editorial board of four journals, a reviewer for 20 others and a reviewer for grant bodies in Australia, New Zealand, South Africa, Israel and Austria. He is Professor of Nutrition at the University of South Australia.

Professor Manny Noakes Manny is currently responsible for Capability Management at CSIRO Animal, Food and Health Sciences and is Stream Leader for the Diet and Lifestyle Programs. Manny has more than 30 years' experience in nutrition and has published more than 100 scientific papers. She has a strong interest in diets for weight management, including the role of protein and other dietary factors in appetite regulation. She co-authored *The CSIRO Total Wellbeing Diet* books and has received several awards for research excellence, including two CSIRO Medals and an Outstanding Achievement Alumni Award from Flinders University.

Pennie Taylor An Accredited Practising Dietitian, she is the Senior Research Dietitian for the Clinical Research Unit at CSIRO Animal, Food and Health Sciences. Pennie also works part-time in a private practice specialising in weight management, bariatric surgery and diabetes care. Her role at CSIRO is to liaise with senior scientists to provide dietetic expertise in developing and delivering designer diets for clinical trials, as well as in analysing dietary data and preparing scientific and commercial publications. Pennie has a strong interest in dietary patterns, nutritional biochemistry and appetite regulation associated with weight-loss maintenance, bariatric surgery and diabetes. Pennie is also accredited by the Joanna Briggs Institute (JBI), an international collaboration of JBI centres in 40 countries focused on evidence-based healthcare and practice.

Other contributors

Associate Professor Grant Brinkworth A senior research scientist and Research Leader of Human Nutrition Studies at CSIRO Animal, Food and Health Sciences, he is responsible for developing and leading several large-scale clinical studies into the role of diet and exercise on weight loss and the prevention and treatment of lifestyle diseases, including obesity, diabetes and cardiovascular disease. He has published more than 50 scientific papers and is an adjunct research fellow at the University of South Australia. He received a CSIRO Medal for Research Excellence in 2005 and the CSIRO Julius Career Development Award for outstanding scientific achievement in 2008.

Dr Conor Delahunty The Theme Leader, Obesity and Metabolic Health for the CSIRO National Preventative Health Flagship, he has more than 20 years' experience in research that underpins and is applied in flavour science, sensory and consumer science and nutritional science. His scientific achievements have application to methods development, food reformulation for health (lower salt, sugar and fat), and demonstrating the role of sensory properties of foods in dietary compliance and eating behaviours, including meal termination. He has proposed and led large multi-disciplinary European Union Framework projects, including the project *Healthy Ageing: How Changes in Sensory Physiology, Sensory Psychology and*

Socio-Cognitive Factors Influence Food. This project involved 24 different research centres and industry who, in collaboration, studied losses of sensory ability that accompany ageing and the effect of these losses on food choice. He also has considerable experience in research management and in engaging with the food and primary production industries. He is internationally recognised in his fields, recently as Co-Chair of the 9th Pangborn Sensory Science Conference, Toronto, 2011.

Professor David Dunstan An ARC Future Fellow and Head of the Physical Activity laboratory at Baker IDI Heart and Diabetes Institute, his research focuses on the role of physical activity and sedentary behaviour in the prevention and management of chronic diseases. He leads the collaborative group that is analysing the lifestyle risk factor data collected from the Australian Diabetes Obesity and Lifestyle (AusDiab) study. He is also the creator of the physical activity program, Lift for Life.

Associate Professor Jennifer Keogh A dietitian with more than 35 years' experience, she is Associate Professor Dietetics and Nutrition at the University of South Australia. She was previously a research dietitian and research scientist at CSIRO's Food and Nutritional Sciences. Her research interests are in the effects of diet on blood vessel function. She has published more than 70 scientific papers.

Dr Lance Macaulay The Theme Leader of Brain Health in CSIRO's Preventative Health Flagship, he has more than 32 years' research experience. His interests lie in understanding the mechanisms of insulin action, diabetes and obesity. He served on the editorial boards of the journals *Endocrinology* and *Frontiers in Bioscience*s. His father had diabetes for 80 years and was one of Australia's longest surviving people with diabetes. This continues to ignite Lance's passion to help other diabetics live long and healthy lives.

Sonia Middleton An Accredited Practising Dietitian who specialises in diabetes management in the Education Services arm of Baker IDI Heart and Diabetes Institute. Her role includes clinical diabetes education, health-professional training, research and commercial projects. In 2009 she was the national trainer for the Reset Your Life Type 2 Diabetes Prevention Program.

Dr Phil Mohr Phil is a senior behavioural scientist at CSIRO Animal, Food and Health Sciences, where he leads research projects for CSIRO's Preventative Health Flagship and CSIRO's Food Futures Flagship. His research into how people reason and make decisions about health, products and lifestyle choices applies his knowledge of psychological theory and methods to the achievement of health-promoting outcomes. He is affiliated with the University of Adelaide and the University of South Australia, and serves on the Social Science Expert Advisory Group for Food Standards Australia and New Zealand (FSANZ).

Professor Merlin Thomas A physician and scientist at Baker IDI Heart and Diabetes Institute, he has published over 200 scientific papers and has received a number of awards, including the 2005 Victorian Premier's Award for Medical Research. He is also a bestselling author of *Understanding Type 2 Diabetes* and *Fast Living, Slow Ageing*. His ongoing research focuses on understanding how diabetes often leads to complications in the heart, kidneys and other sites.

Professor Paul Zimmet AO Director Emeritus of Baker IDI Heart and Diabetes Institute, he has an outstanding international record in diabetes and obesity research. In 2008, he was appointed to the Federal Government's Preventative Health Taskforce. His research in Australian, Pacific and Indian Ocean populations provided new insights into the causes of type 2 diabetes. He is Honorary President of the International Diabetes Federation. In 2000, he led the first-ever national diabetes and obesity study in Australia (AusDiab). Paul has published more than 700 scientific papers, chapters and reviews. He is co-editor of the widely used *International Textbook of Diabetes Mellitus* and *The Epidemiology of Diabetes Mellitus: An International Perspective*.

Index

T

V

W

Y

Z

PENGUIN BOOKS

Published by the Penguin Group
Penguin Group (Australia)
707 Collins Street, Melbourne, Victoria 3008, Australia
(a division of Pearson Australia Group Pty Ltd)
Penguin Group (USA) Inc.
375 Hudson Street, New York, New York 10014, USA
Penguin Group (Canada)
90 Eglinton Avenue East, Suite 700, Toronto, Canada ON M4P 2Y3
(a division of Pearson Penguin Canada Inc.)
Penguin Books Ltd
80 Strand, London WC2R 0RL England
Penguin Ireland
25 St Stephen's Green, Dublin 2, Ireland
(a division of Penguin Books Ltd)
Penguin Books India Pvt Ltd
11 Community Centre, Panchsheel Park, New Delhi – 110 017, India
Penguin Group (NZ)
67 Apollo Drive, Rosedale, Auckland 0632, New Zealand
(a division of Pearson New Zealand Ltd)
Penguin Books (South Africa) (Pty) Ltd, Rosebank Office Park, Block D,
181 Jan Smuts Avenue, Parktown North, Johannesburg, 2196, South Africa
Penguin (Beijing) Ltd
7F, Tower B, Jiaming Center, 27 East Third Ring Road North,
Chaoyang District, Beijing 100020, China

Penguin Books Ltd, Registered Offices: 80 Strand, London, WC2R 0RL, England

First published by Penguin Group (Australia), 2013

10 9 8 7 6 5 4 3 2 1

Introductory text pages 3–13 copyright © CSIRO and Baker IDI Heart
and Diabetes Institute 2013
Text copyright © Penguin Group (Australia) 2013
Photography copyright © Cath Muscat 2013

The moral right of the authors has been asserted.

All rights reserved. Without limiting the rights under copyright reserved above, no part of this publication may be reproduced, stored in or introduced into a retrieval system, or transmitted, in any form or by any means (electronic, mechanical, photocopying, recording or otherwise), without the prior written permission of both the copyright owner and the above publisher of this book.

Design by Lantern Studio © Penguin Group (Australia)
Food photography by Cath Muscat
Food styling by Sarah O'Brien
Recipes by Katy Holder
Food preparation by Tina Asher

Typeset in Parisine Plus and Gotham by Post Pre-press Group,
Brisbane, Queensland
Colour separation by Splitting Image Colour Studio Pty Ltd, Clayton, Victoria
Printed and bound in China by South China Printing Co Ltd

National Library of Australia Cataloguing-in-Publication entry

The CSIRO & Baker IDI diabetes recipe book / CSIRO and
Baker IDI Heart and Diabetes Institute.
9780143568780 (paperback)
Includes index.
Diabetes–Diet therapy–Recipes.
CSIRO.
Baker IDI Heart & Diabetes Institute.

641.56314

penguin.com.au

Acknowledgements

The CSIRO and Baker IDI Diabetes Recipe Book is the result of collaboration between the Commonwealth Scientific and Industrial Research Organisation (CSIRO) and Baker IDI Heart and Diabetes Institute. The following researchers and health professionals have contributed to the ongoing research into *The CSIRO and Baker IDI Diabetes Diet and Lifestyle Plan.*

CSIRO Preventative Health National Research Flagship
Associate Professor Grant Brinkworth, Senior Research Scientist and Research Leader of Human Nutrition Studies
Dr Conor Delahunty, Theme Leader, Obesity and Metabolic Health
Dr Lance Macaulay, Theme Leader, Brain Health
Dr Phil Mohr, Psychologist, Research Team Leader
Professor Manny Noakes, Research Program Leader for Diet and Lifestyle Programs
Pennie Taylor, Senior Research Dietitian, Clinical Research Unit

Baker IDI Heart and Diabetes Institute
Professor Peter Clifton, Honorary Research Fellow
Professor David Dunstan, Head, Physical Activity
Associate Professor Jennifer Keogh, Honorary Research Fellow
Sonia Middleton, Accredited Practising Dietitian
Professor Merlin Thomas, Senior Research Fellow, Head, Biochemistry of Diabetic Complications
Professor Paul Zimmet AO, Director Emeritus

The CSIRO and Baker IDI are grateful to the many other people in CSIRO, Baker IDI and Penguin who have assisted in the production of this book.

The CSIRO and Baker IDI Diabetes Recipe Book makes reference to a number of products and trademarks throughout. Neither CSIRO nor Baker IDI has received financial contributions or other benefits in return for these references from the companies that own these products or trademarks, or from any other entities associated with their promotion.

The information contained in this book is of a general nature. It is not intended to constitute professional medical advice and is not a substitute for consulting with your doctor or other healthcare provider. The publisher, CSIRO, Baker IDI and their employees are not responsible for any adverse effects or consequences arising from the use of any suggestions, preparations or procedures contained in this book.

All matters relating to your health, including diet, medication, and appropriate physical activity, should be discussed with your doctor.